The Monster I Loved

Shannon Clifton

Fortis
Publishing Services

First Edition 2019 Fortis Publishing Services

ISBN-13: 978-1-9163212-1-2

Fortis Publishing
Kemp House
160 City Road
London
EC1V 2NX

This book is a true story. Some names (with an asterisk *) have been changed.

Dedication

I dedicate this book to my son, whom I love dearly.

Acknowledgements

As much as we may fall out, Fiona Oldfield and her lovely family have cared for me since the day they met me, even when it was no longer her duty to care for me. She did! She showed me what having a family feels like. As a child, every birthday I wished for the same thing: to have a family. Fiona made my wish come true. Paul, Fiona's husband showed me what it was like to just have a normal father figure in my life. As for Fiona, she was like a mom and a best friend. With knowing Fiona's background and where she is now, since I was 15 I have always said she is my inspiration.

My thanks also to Kirsten Coxey. For two years she put up with me in my care home. She could have shipped me off to another home at any point just like everyone else did, Kirsten never gave up on me. It's been almost two years since I left and Kirsten still kept in touch and still made sure I was okay. When I was sent to the mental hospital, she was the only one who visited me. The only one!

I thank my writing coach, Ken Scott for all his patience and for being a kind, loving man.

I thank Reinette Visser, my publisher for her patience and for being a nice person.

Ken Scott Biography

Ken Scott collaborated with Shannon Clifton on this book as her writing coach. Ken has written or collaborated on 31 books as author, ghost-writer or writing coach. His book 'Do the Birds Still Sing in Hell' (written with Horace Greasley) has been a Sunday Times bestseller twice since its publication in 2013.

Shannon Clifton
www.fortispublishing.co.uk/shannonclifton

Ken Scott
www.kenscottbooks.com

Letter from the publisher

Dear Reader,

First, thank you for deciding to read this book; we know it's important to young Shannon that her message is heard. She hopes that shining a light on her life can help people who find themselves in a similar position and she also hopes that it can help prevent it from happening to other children. Perhaps the authorities who let her down can learn from her story and not repeat their mistakes.

This book does not, and cannot, contain all of Shannon's telling of her story. It is only the beginning.

Shannon has more to tell and the people in her life have more to tell and in time, it will all come out. Whatever needs to be added will be published on our blog and if you subscribe via Shannon's author page on our website, you will receive an email whenever new material is published.

You may subscribe here:
www.fortispublishing.co.uk/shannonclifton

Again, thank you!
FORTIS PUBLISHING

Contents

Foreword

by Ken Scott

I get enquiries for books on a weekly basis and I was approached by a journalist at the beginning of 2019 who said he knew of a young girl who wanted to share her story with the world. This girl hoped her story would help other people who'd had similar experiences. I picked up the basis of the story, Googled the name Shannon Clifton and read through several articles of how she had suffered at the hands of her father who had been tried, convicted and jailed for some of the heinous offences he had carried out against her.

My immediate reaction was that I didn't want the project, because it tackles the sort of issues that, to be quite honest, I just don't want to talk and write about.

Shane Clifton's depravity knew no bounds and as far as I was concerned, he was in the same league as Fred West or Josef Fritzl and although those two monsters made for fascinating, albeit disturbing reading, did I really want to throw myself into that sort of stomach-churning book?

I have dealt with all sorts of subjects in the past like torture, genocide and murder but such abuse of a child sickens me to me core and it's not something I have ever covered before.

I had a night of sleepless soul searching and felt that Shannon should at least be given a chance to 'sell' her story to me, to convince me that she was committed enough to see out the project. More importantly could she produce a book that not only documents the heartache and pain she had been through, but that could also inspire others? Could she tell them that not only had she survived her horrific ordeal but she had won through and banished at least some of her demons and she was determined to make a success of her life?

That's what I look for in a book; it has to have a happy ending, Hollywood style. I don't think I could ever write a book where the hero dies. That's just me.

I helped Lurata Lyon with her book *The Devil Couldn't Break me* some years back. Lurata lived in Asia at the time and the only way we could work together was via Skype video calls. It was possibly my toughest assignment at that point as over the course of six months she took me through every horrific detail of two kidnaps and incarcerations during the former Yugoslavia war. My main task is to ensure that the subject paints the full picture and that we get all the words onto the pages of the book. Lurata and I both shed many tears as she took me on a journey I could not possibly have imagined. Mass murder, rape, and genocide were commonplace and at one stage, Lurata believed she was about to be murdered and her internal organs harvested for use in Italy and America – sold to the highest bidder. Organ harvesting and the wholesale raping of their enemies' female population were common practice in Yugoslavia at the time – they were the spoils of war. Angelina Jolie headed up a campaign on the subject a few years back and her agent has a copy of *The Devil Couldn't Break me*. Who knows – could it be Angelina's next movie as a director?

With Shannon, I knew that I would once again be taken on another long, unpleasant journey to the depths of despair with many sleepless nights and did I really want that?

I enjoy my job and I have no complaints, but at times in can take me to a lonely, sinister, place but I always bring myself back to reality - it's bad enough for me, what the hell must it be like for the person reliving their ordeal all over again?

I phoned Shannon and she was not what I expected. She was quiet and gentle, delicate even. I had expected someone with quite a tough exterior, brash and ready to speak her mind, but she was not and I wondered if she had the heart or the desire not to mention the determination to tell her tale.

I told her to take a week or two to think about it and to send me a synopsis of her story because I wanted to see the quality of her writing.

She sent me 1,500 words within 24 hours and I knew I wanted to help her. I contacted one of my publishers who agreed immediately to give her a publishing contract and we had a deal.

Without a doubt, the evillest creature on earth is man. And by man, I mean man and not woman. In all the stories and books I have been involved in, the sad, evil, tales I have written about, stories of torture, brutality, death and depravation, the creature known as man was at the centre of everything. Of course there are exceptions and the Myra Hindleys and Rose Wests of this world are out there but they are the exception rather than the rule. As more and more of these stories find their way to me, I am now categorically convinced that more than half of all women have been subjected to some form of sexual abuse by a man.

In the Spring of this year, shortly after starting Shannon's book, I had dinner with an old football friend and his wife and I started to tell them about the content of Shannon's book. I watched as his wife nodded when I passed the comment that there was so much rape and abuse out there. She took a drink of wine and disclosed that she was gangraped when she was seventeen and had never told a soul. Her husband knew, but she had only found the courage to tell him after they had been married for over twenty years. It was a jaw dropping moment and one that still shocks me now. She never told the police or her parents because she was too ashamed. It was bad enough that six men had raped her without the whole world having to know about it. She locked her torment and shame into the deep recesses of her mind and got on with her life. She was one of the lucky ones, she had the strength and determination to fight her demons and get through it, but many do not have the same resolve.

Shannon too, is one of the lucky ones in that she has the strength and determination to get through this. This book wasn't always easy and at times I didn't think we would get it finished. The Monster I Loved is not an in-depth investigation into everything that happened and it doesn't tell the whole story because Shannon is only 19 years of age.

She still hasn't quite processed everything that happened, part of the reason being that she never had any psychological care or decent counselling or therapists who were worth a damn. I got a lot of information from Shannon that she had never told anyone before and yet I didn't want to delve too deeply and I stopped at the entrances to some of the deep, dark corridors of her worst nightmares. Without a doubt, there is more to come out. Because Shannon is so young, it stands to reason that the events in this book happened very recently in her life and she hasn't yet had the healing benefit of the passing of time. The events are still very fresh in the memory of a fragile young girl and therefore I had to tread lightly with the asking of the information and with the telling of the story. This book a work in progress, but it's a step in the right direction and has been very cathartic for Shannon.

I am currently working with two other women. Rachel Kellet and Karen Slater. They are both victims of men's abuse, they are both strong, determined people with a desire to tell their story because it's good for them and they can see their books helping others.

I can't begin to describe my admiration for the women I have worked with recently, it's like a new chapter of my life and for once I have no words to express my gratitude that they have placed their trust in me and decided to take the plunge. It's a brave first step pulling that first chapter together but an altogether incredible achievement when they type out the words- *the end.*

Ken Scott
www.kenscottbooks.com

1

Dysfunctional

Dysfunctional: Not functioning correctly, impaired or abnormal actions; unhealthy interpersonal interactions.

It's an interesting word and quite a recent addition to the English language. It didn't appear in The Collins Dictionary until 1915 and therefore not it's exactly one of those words that stems from ancient history.
I've had the word thrown at me a lot, not at me personally but at my parents, their siblings and even my grandparents. The deeper I delve into the history of my parents and their respective families and the more I uncover some of the horrors within, the more I want to walk away and distance myself from it all to get on with my life.
I´ve tried my best to evaluate the desperate hand that fate dealt me in the early part of my life and I even

moved away from my home city. I couldn´t possibly have stayed there as the memories are too painful and I can´t change the past, so I have stopped trying. I have, however, realised that I have the power to shape my own future and to make it the best future possible.

Every day I wake up and tell myself, 'the best and most beautiful things are still coming my way.' I always keep believing in my dreams and I think it was Eleanor Roosevelt who once said, 'The future belongs to those who believe in the beauty of their dreams.' I hold that quote close to my heart. I believe in beauty and the goodness in people and I can see that in my new foster parents who gave me that second chance that everyone deserves.

As I move towards my bright new future, I´m writing this book and I´m studying towards a university degree in forensic psychology. I chose this course for very personal reasons; I want to know what makes humans act cruel and evil and why we do the things we do. I want to learn how criminals think and how they arrive at the point of acting on their thoughts and committing terrible atrocities that hurt other people. During the six years of this course, I hope to learn why my family members hurt me like they did, especially my father.

Both of my parents come from families who, without a doubt, fall into the category of dysfunctional and I couldn't possibly write this book without telling you a little of my family history.

I won´t cause my family further pain by naming any names as I understand that they´re also victims of their own circumstance and they´ve also suffered enough. They know who they are and what they´ve done to me and I´m learning how to come to terms with it and how to forgive them. Maybe not yet, but perhaps one day. For this reason, all names in my book have been changed.

I want to know why my father did what he did to me and some of the answers clearly lie within his family tree and the actions and consequences of those actions before I was even born.

My mother's family was undoubtably also dysfunctional. My study of psychology brings me to the conclusion that both my parents´ families are about as dysfunctional as it´s possible to be and it makes me think of a study by an American doctor I came across recently. She suggests that in severely dysfunctional families, rape and incest are commonplace. To use her own words, 'where morality and decency are not even an afterthought.'

What is it that makes a family dysfunctional? I believe it's a gradual process, one that spans generations. A family isn't created overnight as a dysfunctional entity and children aren't born with dysfunctionality, but there is undoubtedly some sort of hereditary link. Looking back on my family, there is clearly a pattern of addiction spanning several generations. It´s mostly alcohol, but during the last two generations soft and hard drugs have also played a major part. The children of an alcoholic or a drug addict will likely grow up understanding that the behaviour linked to the addict is quite normal.

All the failings of human nature rear their ugly heads when a parent or guardian is off their face on drugs or continuously pissed out of their brains on cheap wine and vodka. Lack of empathy and understanding, denial, and mental abuse, jealousy, paranoia, inappropriate treatment of others, disrespecting other people's boundaries and controlling behaviour which inevitably lead to violence when the addict finds him or herself in a constant state of chronic anger, coming down from a high or waking up with the mother of all hangovers. And the children look on and think it´s normal.

My father is one of seven siblings and his parents were in an abusive relationship. How they managed to stay together for around forty years is beyond comprehension.

My grandmother owned two flats, one of which she owned with my grandfather and where they lived together. She owned the second flat in her own name and at one point two of her sons lived in it. She ran away to that second flat a lot because of the abuse she suffered from my grandfather. She called the flat her 'go to place.'

She went through hell at the hands of my grandfather and one of the ways she coped was to self-harm. Several times she cut her hair down to her scalp or pulled it out by the roots. She took tranquilisers, anti-depressants and two or three times she was hospitalised because of an overdose. Whether those were serious attempts on her life or a cry for help, no one really knows. I don't suppose she even knows herself.

My grandfather liked to be known as 'the man of the house'; he liked to be in control. It was always his way or no way at all. He got angry over small things like a TV programme he didn´t like or there not being milk in the fridge. He made small things into big things and since my grandmother was conveniently at hand, he lashed out and vented his anger on her. In the early days she fought back, and full-on fist fights developed, but over time she learned that fighting back only made a situation worse, so she stopped.

When my father was sentenced to prison in 2005, I lived with my grandparents for a while. I was very young, but I do remember a few incidents that stuck in my mind. I had only been there a short while when one of my school friends' mums knocked at the door and invited me to a birthday party. I was about five years old and I recall being so excited because I'd never been to a friend´s party before.

On the day of the party, my grandparents started to argue. I remember it just starting out as a bit of bickering, but then their voices got louder and they started swearing. I remember their angry faces and granddad snarling so much that his face turned red. Nana turned to me, 'go into your room for a little while.' I think she just wanted to keep me safe. As I went to my room and sat on the bed, granddad started to shout more and more, louder and louder.

I heard footsteps on the stairs and Nana came into my room. 'Are you okay?' she asked. Before I could answer I heard granddad on the stairs and then he too was in the room and judging by his face he was angrier than ever. Nana sat beside me on the bed. She forced a smile and brushed the hair from my face. 'Are you ready for your friend´s party?'

'Yes Nana.'

My answer triggered a violent reaction from granddad, who started grabbing things from the room. He walked to the top of the stairs and started to throw my Nana's belongings down the stairs.

Nana tried to stop him, but he just kept screaming, 'get out, get the fuck out of my house.'

Nana begged him to stop and ran out of the room and pulled the door shut. As young as I was, I realised it was a sign to stay put. And I did. For five minutes I covered my ears, but the noise still got through. Shouting and screaming again, loud bangs, dull noises and what sounded like things being thrown around. I sat rigid on the bed, so frightened I could hardly breathe and paralysed with fear.

My nana came back upstairs into my room crying; tears were rolling down her cheeks and a trickle of blood ran from one of her nostrils. She sat next to me on the edge of my bed and just held me tight. 'I'm sorry,' she said. I was confused and frightened and I didn't understand what was happening. She stayed with me for a while. She told me I couldn't go to the party and when I asked her why she started to cry again. I was quite upset as I knew all my friends would be there and they'd ask me why I hadn't gone when I went back to school. That concerned me even more than missing the party. It was a chance to be 'one of the gang' and I had missed the opportunity.

My father grew up thinking that fighting and violent behaviour was the norm and violence between the siblings and my grandparents was commonplace. When my father was thirteen years old, my grandfather one day taught him to drive his van. During the last part of the lesson my grandfather explained how to reverse the van onto the drive, but despite several attempts, dad couldn't get the hang of the reverse gear. Granddad told him to step out of the van and before he knew what was happening, he punched my father full in the face, like he would an adult, leaving him lying unconscious on the ground. He locked the van door and went back into the house, leaving my father lying there in a bloody mess for around fifteen minutes before regaining consciousness.

Alcoholism also ran in the family and again, the so called 'normal' behaviour that Dad's siblings witnessed during their childhood and adolescent years affected them badly. One of his brothers was a drug addict and another brother abused, beat and eventually raped his girlfriend. Let´s call her Julie. Julie lived across the road from our family home. She babysat me from four years old and I spent a lot of time with her. As soon as I got to know her, I liked her, and she said I was always asking if could go and see her. As she got to know my extended family of uncles, aunts and grandparents, she became close to one of my uncles. They were about the same age and liked the same things and before long they took an interest in each other and started a relationship.

When I was older, Julie told me, 'he was nice at first but within a couple of months things started to change. The nice, loving boyfriend I once knew became just a distant memory.'

Julie was only fifteen at the time and still at school. She was still so vulnerable, and my uncle took advantage of her. He was a couple of years older and had started working so he had money in his pocket. Julie remembers the first time he hit her. They were out for a drive in his car and he was angry for some reason, but she had no idea why. Without warning he turned on her and punched her in the face. She sat there, shocked and silent, watching as the blood poured from her nose, down her chin and onto her thighs. She started crying and asked him to take her home. On the way home, a police car tried to pull them over.

He obviously realised how bad the scene looked, with Julie bleeding and blood all over the car, so he sped off in fright. The police gave chase with lights flashing and sirens blaring and after a few miles my uncle crashed into a brick wall and came to a dead stop. He was arrested and a police officer told Julie that she was lucky she had been wearing a seatbelt otherwise they would have been scraping her face off the wall. She was sent to the hospital to make sure she was okay. After they eventually returned home, he begged her to stay with him and promised he'd change and never ever hit her again. He asked her to move in with him and he said she was all he had ever wanted. Call it stupid or vulnerable, but Julie believed every word and she moved in.

After a few weeks he went back to his old ways and Julie described him as 'gradually turning into a monster with no control.' One morning Julie woke up and their bed was on fire. At first, she thought it an accident with a discarded cigarette but as she came to her senses, she looked up to see him laughing at the foot of the bed.

As she jumped up, he threw her back into the middle of the bed and made her lie there until he said she could move. The realisation set in that it hadn't been an accident, he had set the bed on fire 'for a laugh.'

Julie was terrified and thought she was about to be burned alive. The fire came closer and closer and he was still laughing, but eventually he decided to put it out with a bucket of water.

It got to a point where she dreaded being at home

with him because the violence all seemed to happen behind closed doors. Leaving the house, with or without him, was always a relief but it wasn´t long before the abuse escalated to a higher level, this time in public.

One day they went shopping together and Julie was enjoying herself because my uncle seemed calm and content. It was a pleasant sunny day and there hadn't been any incidents for quite some time, so she dared to hope that life had turned a corner and he had left his cruel behaviour behind him.

As they walked along, he suddenly moved in behind her and started punching her in the back, for no reason at all. People were watching and Julie hoped someone would intervene and stop him, but nobody wanted to get involved. As they stopped in front of a shop, Julie was crying and begging people to help her, but they all just looked away. She turned around to reason with him, but he hit her again, this time with a bunch of keys in his fist. A small, sharp key caught her cheek and split open the skin. There was blood everywhere and as she pulled a handkerchief from her bag to clean it up, he marched ahead as if nothing had happened. Even then, nobody came to her rescue. She lowered her head and hurried home.

Julie was still in school and her sixteenth birthday was a month away. She called in sick the next day because she was worried that someone would notice all the cuts and bruises on her body. By this time, she was now regularly absent from school and people were starting to pay attention. On both sides of their family people had started to question her about all the marks but, as in nearly all cases of domestic abuse, she made excuses for her man. 'Her man' also preferred her to stay at home where he could exercise full control over her. He claimed that school 'wasn't necessary.'

Thankfully the cut made by the key hadn't been deep enough for stitches, but it took well over a week to heal and even then, she had to disguise it with heavy make-up. She'd been off school for eight days before she plucked up the courage to go back. She got ready early and left after her breakfast. To her surprise he walked out the door with her. 'Where are you going,' she asked, 'you never walk me to school.'

He ignored her as he dropped about twenty yards behind her. It was all rather bizarre. They had been walking no more than a hundred yards when his behaviour took a worrying twist. He started to shout at her. 'You fat, disgusting slag, you worthless fucking whore.' He got louder and viler as they approached small groups of her school friends, 'you ugly fucking bitch, nobody wants you, nobody will ever want you, you're a hopeless piece of shit.'

As she started to cry, he began to push her from behind and when she protested, he started to punch her. She didn't know whether to seek sanctuary at school or run all the way back home but before she could make that decision, she heard a crack and then an excruciating pain in her coccyx. It was agonising and she struggled to put one foot in front of the other. She knew she would never make the journey to school and as she was much closer to home she turned around and headed back. He was smiling. He had his victory.

However, if she thought his triumph would calm him down, she was sadly mistaken. He had another punishment in store for her and this time it was worse than she could ever have imagined. As they walked through the door he started to scream and shout, telling her to get her clothes off. With her eyes filled up with tears she screamed out 'no,' that was the last thing on her mind, but he wouldn't have it and it wasn't the answer he wanted. He took a hold of her hair and dragged her into the bedroom.

'Please stop,' she begged, by now she was screaming out in agony, convinced that she had fractured her coccyx. He almost tore her clothes from her and when she was completely naked, he forced her face down onto the bed. Holding her face down into the pillow she heard him loosen his belt buckle and unbutton his jeans. She prepared to be raped and an in-built defence mechanism told her to stop resisting, it would be over soon and it would be far less traumatic if she let him have his way.

But this was different from anything they had done before. He seemed to be struggling to penetrate her, she felt his rough hands on her buttocks and he was forcing them apart. As he pushed two fingers deep into her anus, she realised the full horror of what he was trying to do to her.

'No, she screamed, 'please God no, anything but that, please I'm sorry.'

Her protests fell on deaf ears and as she screamed out in agony, he penetrated her anally. He pushed and grunted and heaved for what seemed like an eternity until he ejaculated and with poor Julie crying like a baby, he told her to clean herself up and acted as if nothing had happened, as if it a normal part of their sex life and he hadn't done anything wrong. Julie was in so much pain that her body just flopped

onto the floor as she struggled to make it to the bathroom.
My uncle, a fine example of the male species.
My uncle Frederick wasn't much better. There was even an allegation that he raped his own sister but there were no formal charges as the police said it was her word against his.
Another one of my uncles was a paedophile rapist like my father and he raped me when I was five. I write about that incident in chapter seven.

2

Dangerous Situations

My Mother's family was no less dysfunctional and it could be argued that it was a whole lot worse. At one point there were fourteen other children in the house and there were several different fathers involved. One stepdad had fathered 32 children and bragged about it almost daily. Mom's dad struggled with mental illness all his life until he was eventually sectioned and sent to a mental institution indefinitely and my grandmother moved in with his best friend.

Two of Mom's sisters had mental issues and suffered from eating disorders and one of them self-harmed on a regular basis. She became pregnant at a young age and due to ill health she wasn't able to look after her child, who was later adopted.

The other one had her first child at nineteen and just months after the baby was born Social Services got involved as they believed she was putting the baby in dangerous situations. At the time of writing she has had both of her children taken away from her.

Another one of Mom's sisters was rumoured to be a prostitute and from a young age always flaunted herself. She loved attracting attention from boys and men and would boast about her love life on social media. At eighteen gave birth to her first child and word on the street was that the father was only fifteen years of age, although she did admit to cheating on him multiple times so it could have been anybody's.

Her mother once walked in on her having a threesome with two strange men. Her four-year-old son was in the lounge watching cartoons and casually mentioned that 'Mommy was upstairs with two new daddies.'

She charged up the stairs and was absolutely horrified at the site she faced as she opened the bedroom door. She stormed out of the house and called a taxi to take her home and the cab pulled up five minutes later. The taxi driver asked, 'have you just come from that house?' He pointed at the front door.

Her mother was confused and answered, 'yes I have, why, do you know my daughter?'

The driver replied with a grin, 'Oh yes, I know her very well, me and her have had some real good times together.'

Her mother bit her lip; the insinuation was obvious.

The sister had an awful reputation and once admitted to her mother that there could possibly be nine different fathers to her second child.

Another sister was an alcoholic and the situation got so bad my mother had to take her children and look after them until she accepted help.

It gets worse. Two of her brothers were both accused of sexual assault and one of them was also accused of abusing and grooming children. He had just recently been attending court hearings due to the allegations made against him but the case was dismissed due to his mental state. He has a mental age of a child even though he's in his twenties, but some of the family members think he plays on this and they claim they know what he's capable of and that he's perfectly aware that it's wrong and against the law.

He was accused of sexual assault on his niece, aged nine. He has also been questioned about using inappropriate sexual language in front of children and sending sexual voice notes to 11,12 and 14-year-old girls on social media telling them what he wants to do to them and how he was going to have sex with them.

His parents and he had to move away from their home city under police protection after receiving death threats, having their windows smashed regularly and having the words 'Pedo' and 'Nonce' spray painted on the walls of their house.

There is a brother who was accused of violently raping an ex-girlfriend, another who had mental health issues and attempted suicide several times.

Elizabeth*, another sister, had her children taken into care. One child was said to have shown symptoms of having been poisoned - bleeding from the nose and ears and bruising all over the body. The sister is still just twenty years of age and is currently in an abusive relationship with her partner. In a stereotypical world it's seen as the male abusing the female but in this particular scenario I believe they are both as bad as each other. She has been with her boyfriend for around six years and throughout the whole of their relationship there has been nothing but violence and abuse, both physical and mental. Elizabeth fell pregnant with her first child around four years ago and the fact she was carrying a child didn't seem to make any difference to her lifestyle. She still roamed the streets late at night, drinking, smoking, smashing shop windows and getting into fist fights with her younger sister. Just a couple of weeks after her daughter was born, the baby was rushed into hospital because she had suffered some unexplained injuries and struggled to breathe. Social services and the police were called to investigate what may have happened at the family home and her boyfriend was arrested but then later let out on bail. The child was not allowed back home and was instead placed under a care order and sent to stay with her grandparents, where she remains to this day. Elizabeth's second child was also taken into care almost as soon as it was born.

The parents continue to fight for their children in court but both the police and social services advised that as long as Elizabeth remains with her boyfriend there is little chance of getting her children back. The charges against the boyfriend were eventually dropped and Elizabeth remains with him. Both children remain on a care order.

Mum started drinking at the very young age of around eleven or twelve and during the prolonged drinking bouts she became very violent, on one occasion breaking her boyfriend's nose after he had called her a slag. As she entered her teenage years she started getting into trouble with the police and has a conviction for assaulting a policeman. At fifteen she became pregnant with her boyfriend's child. The relationship didn't last long and the birth father was not involved in the child's life. During that pregnancy she also started a relationship with my father and given the two families and track records of alcoholism, drug addiction, rape, incest, violence, suicide and prostitution it was never going to go well. While pregnant with her first child she was still getting into trouble with the police and fighting with my aunties and other friends and sometimes even complete strangers for no reason at all.

Soon after the birth of her first child she found herself pregnant again, this time with me.

3

Repressed Memories

I think it's a natural human reaction to block certain things out and it may seem strange to you, but a lot of my childhood memories are quite pleasant in spite of the horrors I have been through. Psychologists call this *repressed memory* - he ability of our subconscious minds to forget experiences which are so traumatic that they have the ability to send us off the deep end. It helps us cope and stops us going crazy. It toughens us up and something that can seem like the end of the world if it happened to one person, is no big deal if it happens to someone who has to deal with it regularly. Someone like me, who endured horrors worse than any normal person can possibly imagine, learns to cope by blocking it out. It's why a young policeman who attends his first road traffic accident copes worse than one of his colleagues who is approaching retirement and has seen it all before. So, what I'm saying is that I've survived. I've come through and I can look forward to the future and what hasn't killed me has made me stronger. I'm determined to make my life a success; I tell myself I've had a bad start, that's all and I count myself lucky that I have the strength and conviction to put all the unpleasantness behind me and look to the future. Sometimes life throws shit our way and we feel like there is no way out. We feel so stuck and we sit there wondering if there's any point trying to survive.

My early recollections of life were more than pleasant and one of the best memories I have is of the holiday we had in Spain when I was just a little girl. What I didn't know was that this holiday was a result of my mom and dad trying to patch up their explosive relationship after Dad had caught Mom cheating on him and hadn't taken it well.

The story of how Dad found out about Mom's cheating is well known in my family.

It was a warm and sunny day in early May 2004 and Dad said he was going to the pub for a few pints and to watch the football with his dad and brothers. It was a lads only outing; no girls allowed. This bugged Mom, because she wanted to go even though dad told her no. She wouldn't take no for an answer; she was going to the pub and that was final! I remember the day well because I was going to a birthday party at my friend's house and Mom and Dad were arguing about who would collect me if they were both going to the pub.

Dad looked at me, 'I'll pick you up in a couple of hours, behave yourself and have a good time.'

He gave me a hug and a kiss on my forehead and

walked away. I had the time of my life and before I knew it the party was over and dad had arrived to pick me up. My friend gave me a party bag with a piece of her birthday cake and I gave it to dad as a present. As we left the party my father said we were going back to the pub and when we got there, Dad went straight to the bar. He ordered a fruit shoot for me and a pint of Guinness for himself. I couldn't see my Mum anywhere.

Dad asked my grandfather where she was.

'She's gone to the toilet, sit down and watch the football.'

We sat down, but dad kept looking at his watch and started to become quite anxious, looking around to see if he could see my mother.

'Where's my brother?' he asked.

My granddad shrugged his shoulders. 'How should I know?'

Dad tried to watch the football but he was getting edgy and every now and again he stared at the toilet doors.

'Are you sure she went to the toilet?' he asked.

'Yes,' my granddad replied.

Dad stood up and drained the last of his beer. 'Right, let's go and find her.'

I followed him as he stormed over to the toilets and charged through the main door and over to the cubicles. There were five cubicle doors and my father started banging on the only door that was shut.

'Are you fucking in there?'

There was no answer but after a minute of him banging on the door we heard a noise and the door opened. My mother walked out as if she didn't have a care in the world.

'What is bloody wrong with you?' she said as she walked over to the mirror and touched up her lipstick.

I don't know why but I walked into the small cubicle and saw my uncle hiding behind the door.

'Daddy,' I called out, pointing at him. 'Why is Uncle in the girls' toilet?'

I was only about five and I genuinely didn't understand but Mom and my uncle were clearly up to no good. My father walked forward, grabbed his brother by the shirt collar and started to hit him again and again as my uncle tried to protect himself. They were shouting and screaming and ended up on the floor and my granddad and others piled into the toilet trying to separate them while I backed into a corner and started to cry. The bystanders eventually managed to pull them apart and they bundled my dad out of the pub and into the car park but was the worst thing they could have done. The violence I had witnessed in the small toilet area was nothing in comparison to the ferocious cruelty that was about to take place in front of my eyes.

While being dragged out of the pub, my dad spotted my mum over in the far corner of the car park and shouted something about her being a cheating bitch and ran over to her. I watched from the doorway of the pub as they spent a few seconds arguing and then my dad attacked her. He totally lost it and started to punch and kick her. I started to scream and I remember shouting as loud as I could. Mom managed to stay on her feet for a few minutes but the ferocity of the blows was overwhelming and she eventually fell to the ground. By now I was hysterical, because seeing my mom being attacked was entirely different from seeing my uncle being attacked. I thought I was going to be sick. The assault continued and Dad started to kick her in the stomach as she squealed, 'help me, somebody help me!'

Dad stood over her and I could see that her arms and face were covered in blood and she tried to cover her face with her hands. He kicked her hands away and when they fell to her side, he started to stamp on her chest before moving up to her face and head. By now people from inside had heard the commotion and several men ran from the pub and dragged him off. Mom wasn't moving; her eyes were closed and I thought she was dead.

Mom was taken to hospital and ended up with a fractured jaw and other facial injuries which needed stitches. The police were called and dad was arrested, appeared in court and was found guilty. The judge said he would be sentenced at a later date.

Years later I was told by members of the family that my mother had been cheating on my father with my uncle for years. She openly admitted to cheating on my dad and said she had only been in the toilet talking to his brother as he was convinced that he may be my younger sister's father. My sister was at school at the time so the affair must have been going on for at least four years and no wonder dad was so out of control.

After this incident other sordid secrets came to light. While my father was out providing for our family my mother would take us to the Travel Lodge on Nottingham Road. She would order drinks and sit us in front of the TV and then my uncle would arrive and they'd disappear. We thought nothing of it and Mom would say they were just having a drink by the bar. After an hour, sometimes longer she would reappear and we would head back home. There were rumours that she was cheating with other family members too and even one of her own father's friends.

Within a week or two of the attack in which he had fractured her jaw, Mom and Dad made up and resolved their differences. They planned to stay together and by way of a reconciliation they booked the family holiday to Spain, in a place called Calpe, about an hour from Alicante Airport. I can remember being so excited as we drove to the airport and could hardly contain myself as we walked towards the huge plane ready for take-off. The flight was super exciting, because I'd never been on a plane before and I was sitting next to the window so I could look down at all the cities. I remember saying it looked like a play mat with toy cars on. While I was messing about and playing with my brother and sister, Mom was in a mad panic, because she said she hated flying. My father was holding her hand and pulling her hair back from her face, telling her she'd be okay.
When we arrived in the town of Calpe we were dropped off at a small villa with a swimming pool and it was very hot outside. My little sister Chloe and my brother Corrie were so excited and we couldn't wait to explore our new surroundings. We were there a week and I have so many vivid memories. Everything was so clean and tidy; the sky was always blue and Dad cooked most of the food on an open barbeque behind the villa. Mom and Dad seemed happy and there were no fights, no cross words and while mom put Chloe to bed each

evening just as it was getting dark me, dad and Corrie would go in the pool for what seemed like ages. I'd lie on a waterbed and look up at the stars and think how special we all were. I never wanted this life to end.

The villa was on a hill and each day we walked down into the town and explored. We'd walk for ages and get to a big market with lots of flower stalls and it always smelled of fish. We were all hot and sweaty by the time we got there but we still went every day and end up in a small bar for a drink to cool off. On the way home dad would buy a huge bottle of water to carry back to the villa as we couldn't drink from the tap. He carried the bottle all the way back with his shirt off and his shoulders were burnt red raw. Along the way there was a little store that sold lots of different things and I had seen a monkey with Velcro on its hands so they could stick together. I bought it for my dad out of the money my aunties had given me. My dad loved monkeys and he was so happy and hugged me when I gave it to him. I said it was my holiday present for him. Other days we went to a lovely sandy beach, played in the sea and built sandcastles. Dad bought us ice cream and I wished that I could live in that place forever. We were so happy as a family; I can't remember Mom and dad fighting at all.

We also took a trip out to a place called Benidorm, where they had a dolphin show. We sat right at the front and we kept getting splashed as the dolphins jumped out of the water and it was so hot there was a man walking through the stands spraying everyone with cold water from a big barrel on his back. We had our pictures taken with a dolphin and I even got

to touch one. It was strange, like touching a piece of warm rubber covered with sandpaper.
Even at that young age and despite all the dramas that went on around me and the family troubles I knew nothing of, I was happy, I felt special. I was Daddy's little princess, a real Daddy's girl. Little did I know of the terrors that lay ahead of me.

4

Special Treatment

We had a dog at around that time, a Rottweiler Alsatian cross called Rocky. I loved the dog and he was quite protective of our family but he used to chew a lot of things and sometimes if we had people over Dad had to lock him in a shed at the bottom of the garden.

I walked with Dad sometimes at night, when it was dark. There was a park and a field at the bottom of our road and I remember being fascinated by the moon. Dad said it had a face on it and no matter which way you walked the moon's face was always watching you and it followed you wherever you went.

We were part of a huge extended family and in the summer when the weather was warm, Dad often threw impromptu parties. Someone would get on the phone to say there's going to be a barbeque at our house and within the hour fifty or sixty people would pour into the back garden with plastic carrier bags full of beer and wine and sausages and burgers for the grill. He threw one such party a few weeks after we came back from Spain. It was great and again I thought how lucky and special I was to have so many cousins and aunties and uncles who fussed over me because I was one of the youngest. I wanted a party for my fifth birthday but Mom said she didn't have time and it was a lot of money. I was upset because I remembered my friend's party and she got lots of presents and a cake with her name on it. On the morning of my birthday my father took me to Gulliver's Kingdom in Matlock. He took me on lots of rides and bought me sweets and chocolate. I was ever so happy to spend my birthday with my father although I was quite disappointed my mother wasn't there with my brother and sister.

In the early afternoon my father received a call and all I remember him saying is 'we'll come back now.' When we got back home I realised there was a lot of people there. My father picked me up and walked through the house into the back garden where everyone was waiting for me to return. They were clapping and cheering and some were shouting 'Happy Birthday!' and 'Surprise!' I cried when my mother came over and told me she had fibbed - all these people were here for my party; it was my special day. As I walked into the garden I broke out into a big beaming smile. There was a bouncy castle and a bouncy castle slide and there was a table full of party food: sandwiches and sausage rolls and small pies. When my birthday cake came out everyone crowded around me singing happy birthday. It felt amazing having all my friends and family around and everyone was getting on. There were no arguments or disagreements and it felt like a proper family. I thought this is what every day should be like. And yet, the next fight always seemed to be just around the next corner. My mother and father used to fight a lot and my name always seemed to make in into their arguments because Mom was always accusing Dad of giving me special treatment. I have since found out that Dad had his doubts that the other two children were his and that's why I was always his number one, his little princess. He never hid that.

Even at such a young age I witnessed a lot of abuse. There was always tension in the air and it inevitably ended up with one of them throwing a punch at the other. My dad regularly put his fist through doors, he put his foot through the coffee table once and we were always shopping for TVs because dad kept smashing the screens. Sometimes when they had a disagreement it would spill out into the garden and my mother would stand in the front garden screaming and shouting at my father. He would stand there with his hands on his hips demanding that she came inside.

'Get in here now, the whole street doesn't need to know!'

But she wouldn't, she'd stand her ground, almost taunting him to attack her. She'd get louder and louder until eventually he'd snap and go for her and she'd start running around the car screaming as she tried to get away from him. It was as if she almost wanted him to do it, like she wanted the attention from the neighbours.

They got engaged a few times throughout their tempestuous eight-year relationship but thankfully they never got married, because their relationship was built on secrets and lies and infidelity and violence. I often felt like I was a pawn in a chess game because the more arguments my parents had, the more my name was mentioned. My father often took me with him to interesting places and it drove my mother mad that he didn´t include her and my siblings. He would get me anything I wanted, whether it was a gold ring or a pack of sweets.

We'd often go on days out with my grandparents, aunts and cousins and I spent much more time with my father than I ever did with my mother. In fact, the only time I wasn't with him was when he was at work. I remember a day when he came home from work early. Mom had been looking after us and we had misbehaved. It was a sunny day with beautiful blue sky and we were playing in the garden when something happened that Mom didn´t like so she made us stand in a corner of the garden and face the fence. She told us not to move and not to speak to each other. My father came looking for me and when he found me in the garden he told me to get ready because we were going out.

My mother said, 'she's staying where she is, she's been naughty.'

'She's coming with me and that's final,' he said.

My mother started to scream and shout, first at my dad and then at me when I dared to take a step towards him.

'Stay where the fuck you are!'

I froze to the spot.

'Get over here,' dad said and I plucked up the courage and ran over to him. He picked me up and ran out of the house while Mom chased after him calling him the most horrible names. We crammed into the back of my uncle's car with the rest of my dad's family and drove to a funfair where there were lots of rides and my Nana bought us candy floss and lots of sweets. Even though the day started out quite badly for me, it ended with smiles and laughter. I had so much fun with my family but couldn't help feeling a little sorry for my brother and sister who were stuck at home with Mom.

My dad's court appearance for beating up my mom outside the pub was fresh off the back of the holiday to Spain and towards the end of the summer. My parents were trying to patch things up and were actually enjoying a period of relative calm in their relationship at the time. The weather had been nice and there was a party in our garden almost every week.

Life was good.

Then dad had to go to court on a charge of GBH - Grievous Bodily Harm - which is a much more serious charge than common assault or ABH - Actual Bodily Harm. ABH is the usual charge when there's been a fight that's left scratches and bruises and it's clear there was no real intention cause harm. However, because Dad had purposely stamped on Mom's face and fractured her jaw, the charge was Grievous Bodily Harm. Of course he claimed that he hadn't really meant to fracture Mom's jaw and that it was a heat of the moment accident. He also tried to offer Mom's infidelity as extenuating circumstances. His solicitor explained that they had both turned a corner and had settled down with their nice family and I believe my Mom was in court and backed up everything his solicitor said.

The judge took a dim view and sentenced him to twenty-eight months in prison. He told my father he was very lucky because the prosecution had initially considered an attempted murder charge, such was the severity of Mom's injuries and he could have been sentenced to much longer. They took him down to the cells there and then and didn't even allow him to say goodbye to Mom. She took it very badly and suffered a bout of depression that lasted for weeks and during that time she went off the rails.

A couple of weeks after dad was sent to prison she asked my grandparent and a few of my aunties around for coffee. Everything was going well until someone looked out the window and saw Mom climbing into a taxi. We waited and waited but she never came back and her phone was switched off so nobody could speak to her and find out what was going on. Nan and Grandad took us back to their house late that night and Nan put us all in a big double bed for the night. Then the police turned up at the door, because my mother had phoned them and claimed Nana and Granddad had kidnapped us. The police let us stay overnight, but the next morning they drove us back to Mom's.

A few days later Mom was making mini pizzas. I hadn't been feeling great so I went to my room for a lie down and while I walked upstairs I asked my mother to shout when the pizzas were ready. I fell asleep and when I woke up it was dark so I climbed down from my bed and went downstairs, but nobody was there. My brother and sister's bedrooms were empty and the house was all quiet. I was scared to be in the house all on my own and I ran back to bed and cried myself to sleep. Mum turned up the next morning as if nothing had happened and when I asked her where she had been all night and why she hadn't brought me my mini pizzas she simply shrugged her shoulders and said nothing. To this day I don't know where she went that night with my brother and sister.

After my father went to jail I wasn't with my mom for very long. Things weren't the same with my dad gone and I missed him very much and I somehow blamed my mother for everything. Out of the blue, and without any explanation, my mother announced that we were moving to a new house in Matlock. While we were being shown around she asked me a strange question.

'Would you rather live with me or with your father?'

It was a strange question because my father was in prison, but of course I didn't have any concept of what prison was at that age.

I had always been Daddy's little girl so of course the answer to her question was easy.

'I want to live with Daddy.'

She looked at me strangely, nodded her head and knelt on the floor beside me, 'I love you very much,' she said, 'but there's something I have to tell you.'

Right then, I knew my mother was going to send me away somewhere.

5

My Father's First Spell in Prison

I became quite distressed when the family told me that I wouldn't be seeing my father for a very long time. I couldn't understand why not because I knew that Mom went to see him in this 'prison' place and I begged her to let me go with her. I could sense when she was going to visit my dad because she went all quiet and started packing things to take along. I'd keep asking her where she was going and she'd finally admit that she was going to see Dad in prison. I'd start crying. 'I want to go!'

'No.'

'Why not?'

'Because you can't.'

I understand now why they didn't want me to go. It was an awful place, full of bad atmosphere. My nagging eventually paid off and Mom gave in - one day when her and my nana were both going they said I could join them. It took forever in the car and we drove on roads that I had never seen before, but eventually Nana announced that we were there. Nana bought dad some sweets and a magazine at a nearby shop and we walked over to the prison. It was scary to walk into such a horrible place with lots of men in uniform and with keys and locks and lots of people waiting around. There were huge walls and bars everywhere and even at such a young age it didn't feel right. Mom and Nana had to show their passports and empty their handbags and take everything out their pockets. They even checked my pockets and then the man in uniform placed everything into a tub and said we would get it all back when we left. The security check wasn't finished - they patted us down and used a security detector on our bodies. I was in a hurry to see my father and couldn't wait any longer. Why were they doing so many checks? Eventually they led us through to a big room where other families sat at tables, waiting.

Nana pointed to a door and said, 'he'll come through there.'

Sure enough, after a minute or two he walked into the visitors' room. I spotted him and ran over and gave him a hug and told him how much I loved him. He brought me back to the table holding my hand.

I reminded him how much he loved me. 'You haven't forgotten about me, have you?'

'Of course not,' he replied with a huge grin.

That first visit, even though it was in a horrible controlled environment, was very exciting for me. What I didn't expect and couldn't understand was the time limit on how long I could see him. We had no longer arrived than a man in uniform told us our time was nearly up. It was awful.

'Five minutes!' one of them shouted.

And then another, 'Two minutes please!'

People started to get up, kiss their loved ones and leave.

It was a bittersweet experience, but I did love seeing him. Little did I know that first visit would be the best and most exciting, because over time my father's behaviour toward me began to change. I remember always being so excited to go and see him but I never saw him smile as much as he had that first time. He would get angry with me over little things and he wasn't my nice daddy anymore. I started to hate the prison and no longer asked to go, but every now and then Mom and Nan insisted I go with them. I figured it would all be better when Daddy got back home from that awful prison that had turned him so angry.

'When will daddy be coming home?' I asked my Nana and Mom.

'It won't be long.' I didn't know what a sentence was but they kept telling me it wouldn't be long.

Mom told me one day, 'You won't be seeing your dad in there again.'

Great I thought, that suited me fine because he was always angry in there and I wanted my real daddy back. I went to bed that night I thought about how much my dad had changed and the thought that he might have changed for good terrified me, because my life would never be how it used to be. There would be no more fun days out, no daddy and daughter days and no trips to theme parks. I felt quite lost without my father because I'd spent the vast majority of my childhood with him.

My mother had also changed. I felt a hostility towards me and I wondered if she was jealous of the relationship I had with my father. Even during the prison visits it was all about me and him and only occasionally would he talk to her or Nana. At the time her hostility made me think that I was being naughty, because she wouldn't shout at me for nothing but now I realise she just didn't want me. I don't know why and I don´t think I'll ever completely understand. I spent only a short time with my mother and siblings after Dad went to prison and I spent most of my time staying out of her way. I played a lot to take my mind off the fact that my dad wasn't around.

One day my Mom announced that I was going to live somewhere else. I didn't know what to make of it because she hadn't packed any of my clothing and we arrived at the train station with only a small carrier bag containing some sweets and a drink for me. We took the train back to Derby and when we arrived the weather was atrocious. We walked out into the car park at the station and stood waiting. I didn't have a coat and Mom didn't have an umbrella and we stood waiting in the freezing cold. Mum just stood staring out into space until Grandad and one of my aunties eventually turned up in his car. There was an argument between Mom and Granddad and he grabbed me by the hand and dragged me to the car. Mom turned and walked back into the train station. I knew I was leaving Mom and my siblings behind but I wasn't sad; I didn't cry. I was taken to my nana and granddad's house and I remember the day so clearly because my uncles and aunties were all there when I arrived. They all told me how much they'd missed me because they hadn't seen me for such a long time. My clothes were damp and my tiny little socks and huge boots were soaking wet and I sat on Nana's sofa shivering and crying because I was so cold.

'It'll all be okay,' Nana told me, hugging me tightly.

What would be okay, what was she talking about?

I became quite tearful at this point. Everyone was looking so serious and I began to wonder what was wrong with Mom and our new house and deeper thoughts invaded my mind. What if I never saw Mom again, what about Dad and would I ever see my brother and sister again? I had the worst thoughts a five-year-old child could have. I thought my life as I knew it was over and that my family was gone. I was being punished and yet I had done nothing wrong. My auntie made me a small cup of tea to warm my insides and Nana took off my shoes and socks. She rubbed my feet with a towel to dry them and granddad went upstairs to run me 'a lovely warm bubble bath.' I always loved baths, because I thought I could swim in them, just like I had in Spain. When Granddad shouted down that the bath was ready, Nana took me upstairs. She lowered me into the bath and it felt so nice and warm. She used a jug to wash my hair and afterwards she got me out and dried me off with a towel. She brushed and dried my hair and I felt so much better afterwards, so warm and clean. I hadn't felt that way in a long time. When we returned downstairs my aunties and uncles were still there and they started to talk.

'Where have you been?'

'Why did your mother take you away?'

I was confused. 'Mom took me to Matlock, to the

house on the big hill.'

They explained that my mother had kept it a secret and hadn't given anybody the address until recently when she had asked granddad to come and fetch me.

'That's why we haven't seen you.'

'Don't worry,' Nana said, 'you're safe now, you're with us.'

I didn't have the faintest idea what she meant but I picked up that I had a new home now and I wouldn't be going back to Mom's and I was right. Nana and Granddad gave me a new bedroom with a lovely big bed and clean sheets and a thick feather duvet and Nana looked after me and even arranged a new school for me. The school was nice enough but I remember being disappointed that Chloe and Corrie weren't there, which was quite difficult at first. I got used to it though and started to make a lot of new friends and settled in well. After school I'd sit down with my Nana and write a letter to my father telling him how my day was and what I had learned in school. I used to draw him pictures of pretty princesses with huge dresses all coloured in neatly. My nana would also put lots of pictures of me in the envelope before we sealed it and walked down to post it. I came to realise that posting a letter to my dad meant that I would get one back from him. I loved receiving his letters and whenever one had arrived, Nana would have a big smile on her face when I came home from school. I would get so excited and I'd bounce around the kitchen or the living room.

'What does it say, what does it say, can you read it to me, Nana?'

He'd tell me how proud he was of me and how much

he loved and missed me. He'd always tell me how much I meant to him and how I would always be his number one princess. He was never angry when he wrote me letters.

At night, when I lay in bed I'd hold his letters close to my chest with a picture of him and me together. I'd close my eyes and imagine all the good times we shared together and it almost felt as if he was beside me and not angry anymore. I'd just smile in the pitch blackness of the bedroom and whisper, 'I love you Daddy, I can't wait to see you again,' and imagine that he would somehow magically hear my words. I knew deep down that he probably wouldn't but it didn't bother me because I knew that he'd be lying on his bed too and he would be doing exactly the same, holding a photo of me to his chest and whispering how much he loved his little princess. I didn't really miss Mom at first, because everything was great at Nana's house but then things started to change. Nana kept going to hospital a lot and I knew there was something wrong. I was quite mature for my age and had to understand and accept a lot at such a young age, but I didn't quite understand what was going on as nobody would tell me. Grandad came in one evening when I was having my supper and told me that I couldn't live with them anymore. I was devastated and it was such a blow to me and I ran up to my bedroom and started to cry. I was on the move again.

My Auntie came to fetch me. Nana sat at the kitchen table looking sad.

'Don't worry,' she said, 'it's only a few streets away.'

What's wrong Nana,' I sobbed, 'what have I done?'

'Nothing.'

'What's wrong with you?'
She picked up her cup of coffee and walked out of the room.
I went to live with my auntie and cousins and it was another big change in my life. I shared a bedroom with two of my cousins. My bed was small and the bedroom cramped and the rules there were a whole lot different from what I was used to at Nan's. Luckily I could stay in the same school and it was fun for a while, but I knew that I was somehow different from my other cousins and on more than one occasion they told me that I didn't belong there and no one wanted me. On the positive side, they had a big garden with a trampoline and we were also allowed out at the front of the house where we rode our bikes and played cops and robbers, football and kerb. I think I mostly enjoyed being there but some nights I sobbed myself to sleep wishing I was back with my nana and wondering when daddy was coming back. After just a few weeks one of my cousins told me that I couldn't live there anymore and I was going back to Nana's. I went downstairs and asked my auntie if it was true.
Am I moving back to Nana's?'
She nodded without saying anything and went upstairs to pack a case with all my clothes and belongings. Later that day Granddad fetched me and it was back to my old routine. Everything seemed just like it was before. At first. There was a feeling of conflict in the house and Nana and Granddad didn't smile or laugh anymore and they started to argue a lot and shout at each other. I tried not to let it bother me and watched a lot of TV with the sound turned up when the arguing grew louder and louder and I

pretended I couldn't hear them.

My nana would still bath me most nights and I loved to take my toys in the bath. I used to have a fancy shampoo that had a big starfish on the top of the bottle. After my bath I would sit on nana's knee and she would do my hair. She'd brush it all back and I'd laugh and say, 'You're making me look like granddad.'

My nana always treated me very well and I always felt safe there. I had realised by then that my father wouldn't be coming home soon and I tried to make the best of my time with Nana and Granddad until he was eventually let out of prison. Then he would come for me and we would live happily together.

I'd been there no more than a month when Nana gave me that sad look and I knew I was on the move again.

6

Unwanted

This time I moved to the other side of Derby with a different auntie. The car journey seemed to take forever and I was sad as each minute passed because I knew that I was getting further and further away from my nana. The new house was okay but my auntie was quite different from my other auntie as she was still very young and she liked to go out a lot and have fun.

The downside to my new home was that my school was on other side of the city which meant I had to get up when it was still dark to get there on time. My auntie socialised a lot and she took me with her whenever she went over to a friend's house. At first I enjoyed the experience but there would be some really late nights and I was so tired when I had to get up early for school the next day. One day we were at her best friend's house and the friend and her boyfriend disappeared into the kitchen arguing. My auntie looked worried. They got louder and louder and we tried to ignore it until there was a crash in the kitchen and my auntie jumped up and ran through to investigate, but almost immediately she and her friend came running back through to the lounge screaming, with the boyfriend chasing after them with a big knife.

'I'm going to kill everyone,' he screamed, 'every fucking one of you!'

He pointed at my auntie and then me. 'Including those two!'

I had never been so scared in my whole life but they eventually managed to calm him down and he walked back through to the kitchen. I quickly began to realise that my auntie's group of friends weren't very nice. None of them worked and they all sat around smoking strange looking cigarettes and drinking and sometimes my auntie's electricity was cut off when she couldn`t pay the bill. She was seeing a Jamaican man but she was also seeing another man at the same time who lived on the same street as the Jamaican. She was also seeing a third man who'd pick us up from our house and take us to his apartment. She seemed to contact him when she needed money. Her friends joked that she had a lot of boyfriends and it wasn't going to end well.

I eventually had to move school, because she said it was too far for me to stay in the same school. This was quite upsetting for me, because school had been the one stable factor in my life for the last few months, and of course my friends were all there. I went to view my new school with my auntie and I was so sad. They showed us around and I went into my new class for a few minutes. The girls seemed nice, I spoke to a few of them and they were very friendly. I thought it might not be so bad after all. I started at the new school not long after that. My auntie went out and bought my new school uniform ready for my first day and when I turned up for school a nice teacher met me at the gates and told me she would take me to class as it was my first day. I skipped along behind her looking forward to seeing all the new friends I had met the week before and when I got to the classroom I looked around for the familiar faces. They were not there and I didn't recognise anyone.

'This isn't my class,' I whispered timidly to the teacher.

She pointed at a seat. 'Sit there.'

And then she left.

I was confused. At break time when everyone went out to play, I saw the kids I had met the previous week. We were separated by a big black fence.

They called over to me, 'You're in the wrong year!'

I called a teacher over and told her, but she walked away. I kept telling my auntie over the next few days that I was in the wrong class and it took a while for anyone to listen but then they finally realised and changed my class. After this little mistake I settled in well and made great progress, especially when it came to reading and writing, which were my favourite subjects. I made new friends, I mixed well and I was particularly close to one of the neighbour's sons who was in my class. We became best friends in and out of school until one day my auntie told me the news that he was leaving the area and I was very

upset. He too was rather sad that he had to move away and go to a different school.
I asked my auntie when I would see him again.
'What do you mean?' she asked.
'When will he come to see me?' I asked innocently
'Not ever,' she said, 'he's moving south, why would he want to come and see you?'

I couldn't get my tiny head around that. I expected her to say we would see each other in the holidays or an odd weekend.
'No,' she said, 'he's moving hundreds of miles away, because his dad has a new job, so best just forget about him and find a new friend.'
For the last few days we spent as much time as possible with one another. I told him we would meet up again and he said that would be nice. We could play games and read together and watch the cartoons on TV.
I never saw him again.

There were times when I felt just like a child and I did all the normal things a child would do. Then other times it wasn't so great, because there was a lot of conflict and things going on that a child should not see. My auntie was always complaining about money, or rather the lack of it but as one of her friends shouted at her one day, 'you always have enough money for weed!' I now knew that weed was those funny shaped cigarettes that adults smoked and that it made them feel good but it made the house stink and gave me a headache. My auntie was so desperate for the money to buy weed that she sometimes forgot to buy food. Sometimes the electricity and gas would go out and we would sit in the dark, freezing cold and hungry while she sat in a corner wrapped in a blanket smoking the funny cigarettes, seemingly without a care in the world. We also had a TV with a box on the back and you had to put Pound coins in to keep the programmes on. It sometimes went off when I was watching the cartoons and I'd ask her for another Pound.

'I've got no money,' she'd say as she blew out the smoke from her weed, 'go and ask the neighbour for a quid.'

I would run next door to the neighbours and beg them for a Pound coin. The neighbour would shout at me, 'She's enough money for weed, tell her to fuck off.'

It wasn't so nice living with my auntie.

'Go and run a bath for your cousin,' she told me one day.

My one-year-old baby cousin was staying with us and I felt all grown up to be given the responsibility to run her bath. I was five years old. I managed to get the taps to turn on although one of them was very stiff and I filled the bath and put some bubbles in and called out to my auntie that it was ready. She came up the stairs, undressed my cousin and lowered her into the bath. My cousin started screaming. She screamed so loud my auntie dropped her into the water and that made her scream even louder. In a mad panic my auntie lunged for her and then found out what the problem was. I hadn't put enough cold water in the bath and it was absolutely scalding. At five years old I don't think I really knew what temperature a baby's bath should be. My auntie was shouting at me as the baby continued to scream and I noticed that her little body had turned bright red.

'What's wrong?' I cried. 'What is it?'

'You stupid little cow!' my auntie screamed back as she ran out of the bathroom.

'Stay there,' she called out, 'I'll be back.'

I was standing in the hallway when she reappeared and she dragged me back into the bathroom. She was furious and wild looking and as she pulled me towards the bath and plunged my hand into the hot water. I had never felt pain like that before and I screamed out in distress, pulling with all my might to get my hand out of the water but she held it firm as she slapped me across the back of the head with her other hand.

Despite my protests and screams and the buckets of tears I cried she held my hand in the water for a long time while she lectured me on the dangers of hot bath water.

I felt sure that the skin would be falling off my hand when she eventually lifted it out. The skin was red raw and small blisters were starting to form on the back of my hand and the pain went on and on. I wanted to touch it and rub it better but I somehow knew that would be even worse. When my auntie left the bathroom I plunged my hand into the cold water of the toilet bowl and the pain eased a little. I held it in there forever. I never wanted to suffer pain like this ever again and I told myself I would never run a bath for as long as I lived.

7

Our Little Secret

My father wasn't the first man to rape me.

Not long after the incident with the bathwater a family member came to live with us. Let's call him Steve*. He was about eighteen or nineteen years old and great fun. He'd take me out in his car and I made my mind up that he was my favourite family member. He would spoil me and buy me presents and take me out to the park. He had a girlfriend but not long after he came to live with us, they broke up and he was sad. A few weeks after they broke up we went to a fun fair and she was there. She asked me if I wanted to go on a ride with her but because I thought Steve didn't like her anymore, I said no. She pleaded with me but I flatly refused, hanging onto Steve's trouser leg.

Steve got a phone call when we arrived home to say that his girlfriend had been in a car accident. He rushed out of the house, climbed in his car and drove over to the hospital and when he came back a few hours later and told my auntie she had died. To this day I wish I'd gone on the ride with her so I could have had the memories of her gorgeous smile. Perhaps if I had gone on the ride with her she wouldn't have been in the wrong place at the wrong time and I feel was my fault that she died. As a five-year-old child I was experiencing guilt for the first time. My uncle didn't take his girlfriend's death very well but he still he started a relationship with a very young girl almost immediately. She was still at school, in year nine and she was thirteen years old. He would meet her after school in his car. When he fetched her from her house he sometimes took me with him and made me knock on her door. I thought nothing of it at the time, but looking back at it now it was clearly because he was a lot older and obviously her parents weren't happy about it.

I shared a room with my Steve and it was a great big adventure and I loved it. One morning I woke up in a jolly mood, got down from my bed and made my way over to the other side of my room where Steve's bed was. He was lying there fast asleep and I got onto his bed and began to jump up and down.
'Get up, c'mon time to get up!' I tried to pull his covers off and I was laughing and shouting, 'get up, wakey wakey lazy bones!'
Sometimes in life you block out things that are unpleasant, things you try not to remember. But I guess even though you can block some things out, there are other things that happen that are so horrific and painful it's almost impossible. Steve wasn't best

pleased about being woken up and as he grabbed me by both hands there was something different about him, a strange look in his eyes that I had never seen before. It was all so confusing and I didn't have any understanding of what was happening. He started touching my face, gently, and then moved his hands down to my shoulders and my stomach.

'What are you doing, stop it,' I said.

He placed his finger across his lips, 'shh…' he said, 'it will be our little secret.'

What secret, what was he talking about? His hands were rough on my soft skin, I remember his fingernails were dirty against my pale white skin.

He was unbuttoning my pyjamas.

'Please stop,' I said.

I reached down to stop him but he pushed my hand away forcefully.

'Our secret,' he whispered in my ear.

For the first time I noticed that he was naked and there was a horrible looking thing sticking out between his legs. He was climbing on me, pushing me onto the bed and his hands were between my legs. I knew something was wrong, I didn't know what but something was terribly wrong. I begged him to stop but he kept pushing something between my legs. His face had changed. This wasn't Steve; his face was twisted and sweat stood out on his brow and I could smell his rank, stale breath. He pushed hard and the pain shot through me like nothing I had ever felt before. Before I could scream a heavy hand clamped across my mouth and he started to push again. It was like a knife stabbing me time after time.

'Our secret,' he kept repeating, 'we can't tell anyone, if you do they will send you away to live with strangers and you'll never see your mom or dad ever again.'

When it was all over he cleaned up the blood. I couldn't move; I couldn't stand. I crawled back to my bed on my hands and knees and pulled myself up on the bed. Every twist, every turn, every slight movement of my body was sheer agony. I lay on the bed for the rest of the morning sobbing, sure I was going to die. I lay in bed for the whole of the day, scared to move in case I started to bleed again. My auntie brought me some lunch upstairs, but I couldn't eat it. She asked me what was wrong but I remembered what my uncle had said about the secret.

I shook my head. 'Nothing.'

My uncle disappeared for the rest of the day and that night he came into the bedroom and fell asleep as usual without saying anything to me.

He woke me the next day. 'C'mon' he said, we need some breakfast and then we're going out.'

I did as I was told and I didn't cry.

We went around to his thirteen-year-old girlfriend and he got me to knock on her door and we carried on as normal. Everything was normal. I don't know if he ever raped or abused me again, because I can't remember. Perhaps I have blocked it out, I just don't know.

8

The Bitch

I now realise that people change and sometimes they change so much that they become different people. As a five-year-old visiting my dad in prison I was very confused. My mom had change and her feelings towards me were clearly different from what they once were. On each visit to the prison I could see that my dad was also changing. What hurts deep inside is when all the good in a person becomes a distant memory and I wonder what happened, is it my fault, was I to blame. More than that, I wonder if I must change myself in order to get back the person I once loved. Gradually, over time, both my mom and dad were completely unrecognizable. What I didn't know at the time was that my dad was slowly changing into a monster. I idolised my father but I began to get the distinct feeling that at times he just didn't like me. It was the way he sometimes looked at me the same way my mom looked at me, as if she didn't care, as if I were a nuisance, a pest. To all intents and purposes, she had abandoned me and it hurt. Even at such a young age I knew she didn't want me, but I clung to the hope that my dad would never change. He would always want me, because I was his little princess. I was his world and he was mine. As soon as he got out of this horrible prison my life would return to normal and Dad and me would live together and he would never send me to my auntie's or Nana's again. It would be just Dad and me forever. During those first two or three visits he seemed just as excited to see me as I was to see him. However, there were other times when he seemed disinterested, as if he wasn't so pleased to see me and he would glare at me and make me sad. How could this be? I was his daughter; I was his princess.

During some of those visits I wondered if my father even loved me and prayed with all my heart that he would get out of prison so that I could have my old Dad back, the one who used to love me so much. Whenever Nana or the family were around the visiting table he would smile and stroke my hair and tell me that he couldn't wait to get out so that we could all 'get back to normal.' I usually visited with Nana and my aunt and my baby cousin and after a while they would wander over to the soft toy play area with my cousin and my father and I would end up being alone.

'When did you last see your Mom?' he'd ask, and his face would change. His smile would be replaced by an angry look. Whenever he mentioned my mother there was always an angry look on his face.

And I'd ask in all innocence, 'have you had another

fight?'
'No,' he'd snap back.
And he'd start to question me 'Where did you meet her, who was you with?'
I'd tell him, 'I met her last week, with Auntie and my cousins, we went to a park and played on the swings.'
'Last week?'
'Yes,' I said, 'Wednesday I think.'
And Dad would swear and bang his fist on the table as if he didn't want me to see Mom. He would take his frustrations out on me and say horrible things.
'You little bitch, you fucking slag.'
He used the slag word a lot and he would swear at me as if he was swearing at an adult.
'You love your Mother more than you fucking love me.'
'No,' I'd protest, 'I don't.'
'You are betraying me.'
'I'm not Daddy.'
I had to take sides all the time and it was always so confusing. Why did they make me do this? I never knew if I was coming or going with either of them. When I was with Mom, she'd ask the same silly questions. A pattern began to form, and life eventually consisted of three separate bubbles. My home bubble, my visiting Dad bubble, and the bubble I was in whenever Mom was on the scene. It was like separate worlds; a game that I'd have to play to keep the adults from shouting at me and turning nasty.
I knew Mom visited dad in prison and sent him letters and that they phoned each other. Dad would tell me when I visited him, and I began to sense

exactly when they had been fighting or if she hadn't visited him for a while, because that's when he was angry and shouted at me and turned nasty. That's when he would ask me the horrible questions.

My mother was almost completely out of my life at this point, yet whenever I did meet up with her, I sensed that these were the times she had had a fight with Dad. She would contact my aunt and say she wanted to see me. My father would be livid but being in prison there was nothing he could do to stop it.

'Your mother is playing fucking games,' he'd snarl at me when we were alone in the prison. 'Tell your auntie not to let her see you.'

I sometimes wondered if it would be better to lie and tell him I hadn't seen her, but she was my mom, why couldn't she see me? I didn't understand. My Auntie never stopped my mom from coming to the house. She was younger than Mom, still only a teenager herself and she didn't quite understand everything that was happening either. My aunt wasn't mature enough to see through the games my parents were playing.

I didn't understand this at the time, but I realise now that my parents only thought about themselves and that I was an insignificant pawn in a game of adult chess. They didn't consider my wellbeing at all and I was simply a pawn in their game.

I began to worry about my brother and sister. I didn't see them very often, because my mom nearly always came to visit me on her own.

I'd ask her where Chloe and Corrie are.

'Couldn't come.'

'Why not, Mom?'

'Just couldn't.'

I missed them terribly. Mom had given me away and separated me from my siblings. I felt abandoned and I missed them so much. How did my mother explain that to them? It must have been devastating for them. We had spent years as a family then suddenly my father went to prison and a few weeks later Mom sent me away. It was hard enough for me to comprehend, what on earth did my three-year old sister Chloe think? My brother was a little older, he was seven. What had she told him about the mess our family was in?

Mom was in and out of my life while Dad was in prison. Apart from her visits to my auntie, we would sometimes all meet up in town and go for food. My auntie and cousins would join us and sometimes Mom would my brother and sister. It was good to see them, and we would begin to bond as siblings again. For a while we'd meet every week and it was great fun and we were almost normal again.

Then suddenly, all contact stopped completely. My Auntie would tell me that Mom didn't want to meet up and didn't want to see me. How could this possibly be, what had I done to upset her? Why did she keep doing this? My mother was in and out my life like a yoyo.

I kept asking my Auntie, 'why does Mommy not want to see me?'

'I don't know Shannon.'

'Does mommy not love me anymore?'

She'd shrug her shoulders. 'I'm sure she does.'

'Am I ever going to see her again?'

'Of course, you are.'

'When am I going to see Chloe and Corrie?'

Time and time again my auntie had to sit me down and explain that she didn't know why my mother kept doing this to me and she couldn't explain why she kept letting me down and disappearing out of my life. It got to a point where I felt as if my mother had destroyed me and at such a young age I felt completely broken. I was confused and lost and I felt unloved and unwanted and was unable to understand what was happening in my life.

I had heard my Nan and Auntie talking about suicide and I wondered what that was. Nana had a strange calm look on her face when she talked about suicide with my auntie and she said she was broken and it would take away the pain. I wondered if suicide would take away my pain and how I would go about it. I walked into the bathroom one day and Nana was sitting on the floor with a pair of scissors. She looked pale and there were clumps of hair on the bathroom floor.

'What are you doing Nana?' I asked.

'Go away. Leave me alone.'

She brought the scissors up to her head and cut a huge chunk of her hair and threw it onto the floor.

'No! Nana,' I screamed.

'Fuck off and go away.'

I ran over and pulled the scissors from her and she started to cry. She wiped the tears away and then looked strangely peaceful. She reached up to her hair with her hand and took a huge handful of hair and pulled it.

'What are you doing Nana?'

I knew what she was doing, she was trying to pull her hair out.

I cried out for her to stop but she kept yanking harder and harder until eventually the piece of hair came away from her scalp. And then that peaceful look again.

This was my first experience of self-harm, but it wouldn't be my last and it wasn't always as passive. I caught Nana in the bathroom with a pair of scissors again a few weeks later and again she was determined to take out her frustration on her hair and scalp but this time she was more violent and cut indiscriminately at her hair. I noticed the blood on the scissor blades and a small pool on the bathroom floor. I screamed and Nana looked up. There was blood all over her face and yet she had that strange peaceful look again.

My auntie cut her wrists in front of me one day. She was self-harming too. It was just another crazy day in the fucked-up world that I was living in.

As children we copy what our peers do so it was just a matter of time before I tried out self-harming for myself.

I think I was six years old and by now I had seen Nana and Auntie self-harm about a dozen times. Auntie favoured cutting her arms and wrists with a razor, but Nana always went for her hair and more often than not she didn't bother with the scissors or a knife but simply grabbed fistfuls of hair and tore it out at the roots. I didn't really fancy ripping my hair out, because I was quite fond of the way I looked so decided to go for the razor option. I walked into the bathroom one day and went to the cabinet where Auntie kept the razors. I took one out of the little pink packet. I looked at it and wondered where the blade was and how I was going to cut myself. I was looking at a safety razor and the three small blades were surrounded by pink plastic with a little soft gel strip at the top. I remembered what my auntie had done when she had cut herself so I pressed the face of the razor into my wrist and started to slide the blade back and forth. Nothing happened. I looked down at my wrist where the blade had been and there were a couple of indentations in the skin but no blood. I tried again, this time I pressed the blade in harder and deeper. I pulled it back and forward and then yelped as the blades bit into my flesh and a searing pain hit me.

'Ow that bloody hurt,' I cursed out loud as I looked down and saw the blood.

I didn't like it. All that blood. No, this was no fun. The last time I remembered seeing that much blood was after my uncle had raped me and I bled between the legs. By now my wrist was throbbing and the blood was dripping onto the floor. No! this wasn't for me, just what did Nana and Auntie get out of it? As painful and unpleasant as that first experience of self-harm was, I would return to it in my teenage years.

During the time my father was in prison I don´t think I had any positive role models. I began to realise that nobody really wanted me and that's why I was being passed around from one family member to another. It sometimes felt like they all did things to hurt me on purpose and yet I know they all loved me in their own dysfunctional ways. One thing they did do to me during that time was to paint my mother as some sort of monster who had abandoned me and sent my father to prison. They made me believe everything that ever went wrong was my mother's fault. They got me to start calling her the Bitch instead of Mom and as a five-year-old I went along with it. They started to correct me every time I said Mom.

'It's not Mom,' they would say, 'it's The Bitch.'

'The Bitch,' I'd repeat, and they'd laugh and because they were laughing it felt good to call her 'The Bitch' and for a while it stuck. My dad's sister said a lot of negative and spiteful things about my mother and then take me to see her and completely change. She'd smile and they'd laugh together and it was as if they were the best of friends but back home, she would be The Bitch again and Auntie wouldn't have one nice thing to say about her. I had one ray of hope and that was to wait for the day when Dad would finally get out of prison.

Towards the end of my father's sentence I couldn't wait to see him walking out of that horrible prison. As the days drew closer, I was extremely excited to see him and the thought of knowing he was coming home had a profoundly positive impact on me and I was so much happier within myself. My nana was rather excited too and she planned a small welcome home gathering for him with the family. Every morning for the last couple of weeks before his release I'd wake up and bolt down the stairs.

'How many days till daddy comes home?' I'd ask.

She'd grin, 'just ten days to go.'

The following morning, 'just nine.'

Eventually it came to the day of his release and my excitement and happiness were indescribable. Knowing my father was going to be with me in just a matter of hours was beyond description. We would be a normal family again and everything would work itself out and I'd see Chloe and Corrie every day. Daddy would wave a magic wand and make everything right.

There would be no more time restrictions and no prison guards or scary looking men sitting at the tables beside us. Daddy wouldn't get angry and my parents wouldn't fight or play games. I convinced myself that prison had been to blame for all the bad things in my world and especially that it was the reason why Mom didn't want me.

I woke up early and ran downstairs. 'How many days Nan?'

'None!' she shouted. 'Today's the day!'

I ran around the kitchen excitedly with my hands waving around above my head.

'I need to look pretty for when we pick Daddy up.'

Nana was smiling, 'I'll do your hair. And here, this is for you.'

She handed me a pretty new dress she had bought the day before. I snatched it out of her hand and ran upstairs to get ready. My Nana had arranged to pick him up from the prison and we went with my auntie. It was a rather long drive so on the way there we decided to get breakfast at a fast food restaurant. I remember not eating very much as I just wanted to get to the prison as quick as I could. As we finally arrived there we waited at the gates and I was thinking how he would walk through the gates any moment now and could hardly contain my excitement.

We waited and waited and waited.

We watched as the gates opened and a few men walked out. I strained to get a look but couldn't see Dad anywhere. We waited so long we had all began to get agitated and Nana and Auntie started to argue when Auntie wondered if we had the day wrong. An hour later Nana decided she wasn't waiting any longer and rang the prison from her mobile.

I heard her shouting at someone, 'he should have been out bloody hours ago!'

They didn't seem to want to give too much information, but she was raging on the phone and demanded to know what was happening.

'He's done what?' she bellowed into the phone.

She ended the call, cursing and swearing at whoever was on the other end of the line. And then my world came crashing down. She told me there had been an incident on the prison grounds.

'When is he getting out?' I asked innocently.

She lit up a cigarette and blew the smoke high into the air.

'The stupid bastard,' she cursed out loud.

My father had stayed out of trouble throughout his sentence and when he was ready to be released, he had managed to get himself into a silly fight with some other inmates.

'When is he coming home,' I repeated.

Nana didn't answer.

My Auntie took me by the arm and turned me away from the prison gates.

'C'mon, let's go home.'

'Are we coming back tomorrow?' I asked.

'No.'

'Then when?'

She turned to face me. 'I don't know, nobody knows.'

In the car on the way back my nana and auntie were talking about how it would be months before he would be released. I was devastated to hear my father wasn't getting out and I sobbed most of the way home.

'I just want to see daddy,' I whispered to myself under my breath, 'I just want to give him a big hug and tell him that everything is going to be good again.'

9

Released, Just Me and Daddy Now

I spent the next two months alternating between living with my nan and with my auntie.
I asked about my Dad constantly, 'when is he coming home?'
'I don't know.'
'Why don't you know?'
'We just don't know, nobody knows.'
I couldn't get my head around it. I had been looking so forward to the moment my Dad walked through those prison gates when he would surely sweep me up in his arms and now there was nothing. No Dad, no hugs, no kisses, no 'I love you princess,' no release date. I wondered if he was going to be locked up forever.
'When can we visit him?'
'We can't, now shut the fuck up and drop it.'
I was eventually told that my dad had got mixed up

with the wrong crowd and got himself involved in a mass brawl that resulted in one of the inmates being hurt badly. Everyone who had been involved had time added to their sentence and Dad had two months added to his.

I was living with Nan and Grandad and one evening they put me to bed at around eight o'clock, which was early for me. It was a school night and I had been tired but I heard a knock on the door and wandered downstairs, half asleep.

I heard voices in the kitchen and walked in. There he was.

He smiled, 'hello Princess.'

I ran and leapt into his arms and he swung me around and around. He smothered me with kisses and his smell was just as I remembered. Grandad was asking him how he got home but he said it didn't matter.

'I'm home now, that's all that matters.'

He looked at me, 'I can be a father again.'

Nan didn't seem happy and she kept asking him how he got home, because they would have fetched him as the prison was miles away.

'It doesn't matter,' he repeated, 'I'm here to stay and that's what counts.

'Stay with me daddy, stay in my room.'

He turned to me, 'I can't Princess, I have to get back.'

'But…'

It turned out Dad had a curfew and he had to be back at a special probation hostel. My joy was short lived though he did stay for more than an hour and when he left he promised he would be back in the morning to wash and blow dry my hair. And he was. He was there for breakfast and after breakfast he bathed me and washed my hair and blow dried it. I had my daddy back and I didn't care that he had to sleep somewhere else because he promised it would only be for a short while and he would still see me every day. After a couple of weeks I moved back in with my auntie as her house was nearer to the hostel and true as his word my dad came every morning and washed and blow dried my hair. Mom was seeing someone else at that time and dad was sometimes very angry about it. As part of his bail conditions he wasn't allowed to see her as she had been the person he had assaulted and there was a restraining order against him. They still met up though. They met in town and sometimes at my auntie's and I wondered if perhaps one day we would be a family again. I didn't like moving from house to house and I didn't want Daddy to leave at night when it was dark, and I wanted to see my brother and sister again. I was in town one day when Mom met up with Dad. They were both nervous but seemed happy to see each other. Dad explained that if they were spotted together he would go back to prison and I didn't want that.

'Keep a look out for police cars Princess,' Dad said.

'What?'

'Just shout if you see a policeman.'

I wandered to the street corner as Mom chatted with Dad in the middle of the street.

'Police!' I shouted as I spotted the car edging its way up the high street.

I'd never seen Dad move so fast as he grabbed Mom's hand and dragged her behind a huge doughnut truck. He looked so relieved when the police car moved slowly by and gradually disappeared. Sadly, it wasn't the fairy story I thought it would be because Dad started to change and when he and Mom met, they rowed more and more often. There was never any violence, just angry voices and he kept accused her of cheating on him while she countered with 'what did you expect?' Dad started to miss more and more mornings at my auntie's house and when he did turn up he lost his patience with me all the time. He used to spend hours with me, especially at the weekends and nothing was too much trouble, but now he would come to brush and blow dry my hair and within ten minutes he was away. He'd get angry if I didn't sit still and then he'd leave, telling me he had someone to see or he had a 'business meeting'.

One day I wouldn't stop moving my head from side to side, because there was a cartoon on the TV in the bedroom and I wanted to see it.

'Keep still,' he said.

I moved.

'I'm warning you.'

I moved again.

I felt of a movement of air, and I saw his hand above his head, but I was caught completely off guard when he smashed the hard-plastic hairbrush down into my skull and I slipped to the floor. I blacked out and when I came around I was lying on the bed with a blistering headache and my auntie was standing over me, screaming at my dad.

'Get the fuck out of here and don't come back!'

Dad stood with his hands on his hips and shouted back that he had hit me because I wouldn't sit still. He left soon after.

I had an enormous lump on my head but luckily the

brush hadn't split the skin and I didn't need to go to the doctor. My auntie sat with me with a bag of frozen peas on my head. Although the physical pain subsided quite quickly that feeling of betrayal was harder to shake off. Why had he done that? I'd only wanted to watch a cartoon. It was the first time my dad had been violent towards me, but in the following months and years it become a regular occurrence.

Auntie announced that I could no longer stay with her. What had I done to upset her? It wasn't long after the hairbrush incident but surely she couldn't blame me for that. Dad took control of the situation and used it to his own advantage. He contacted Social Services and told them what was going on. He said that Auntie didn't want me to live with her and my Mom didn't want me either. Even though he was still in the hostel and under the conditions of his bail, he persuaded the authorities that he was the only member of my family who wanted me and demanded the authorities provide somewhere we could live together. He demanded the right of a father and daughter to be together.

He came over as a loving, caring father and he conned everyone. The authorities provided us a room in a DSS bed and breakfast establishment in Derby. It had two beds and a shared bathroom outside in the corridor. Whenever I wanted the toilet or to use the shower Dad stood guard outside the door to make sure nobody came in. Despite there being ants everywhere, it was pleasant enough and the people who ran it appeared to be nice. While I didn't know it at the time, it would be the beginning of nearly ten years of unimaginable horror, because it brought out the monster in my dad.

My dad was now almost always angry and he didn't call me his Little Princess anymore. Mom had a new boyfriend and Dad wasn't happy about that at all. She had tried to move on and that didn't suit him because he wasn't in control of her so I think he started taking out his frustrations on me. Looking back, it was a ridiculous environment in which to live. We were cooped up in a small room with nothing but a television. There was no room for any toys and not even a kitchen or a separate bedroom to go to for some alone time. We were in each other's hair 24 hours of every day and Dad once told me that conditions in the prison were better than where we were living now. Dad began to hit me more and more often. He slapped me mostly, across the face and across the back of the head and he began shouting at me and pulling my hair, telling me everything was my fault. Within a few weeks I grew to hate the place and I convinced myself that it was our prison cell and it was responsible for the way dad was and I prayed that we wouldn't be there long.

We were there for nearly six months.

10

Stop It Daddy, I Don't Like It

The council eventually moved us into a one bedroomed flat and I was elated. I finally saw Dad smile and on the day we moved in I was so excited when I saw my bedroom. There were already some toys in it and a small bed in the corner. It was tiny but it didn't matter, I had my own room and my own bed.

The family arrived with pots of paint and brushes and paste tables and rolls of wallpaper and for two or three days they all pulled together and I was amazed at the transformation of that small grotty little flat. Suddenly we had a clean, nice smelling home and I hoped in my heart of hearts that daddy and I could start again. While Dad appeared happier in our new house there was always another drama around every corner. Mom announced she was pregnant by her new boyfriend and dad went ballistic. His slaps turned to punches and he's punched me for little or no reason. I was playing in the kitchen one day. I had a tiled floor and I had marked out a little hopscotch court with chalk. I had a small pebble that I threw onto each square as I hopped on the tiles to retrieve it. I had been hopping and skipping for about five minutes when he stormed into the kitchen.

'Don't you know how to fucking keep quiet?'

'But…'

'I'm trying to read the paper and all I can hear is you and that fucking pebble on the tiles.'

Before I could answer he propelled his fist forward and instinctively I ducked, I wasn't quick enough, and his fist caught me square in the forehead. I flew across the room and smashed into the kitchen unit below the sink where I sat in a daze, looking up at my dad while he stood over me.

'You fucking little bastard, it's all your fault. I'm going to teach you a lesson.'

And he was gone. I tried to stand up, but my legs were like jelly and I sank back to the floor. I could hear Dad in the bathroom; he was running a bath. Why was he running a bath? It was early morning, nobody took a bath in the morning, we bathed in the evening.

He was back into the kitchen, grabbed me by my long hair and started dragging me across the tiles. I begged him to stop; the pain was excruciating, and I thought he was going to pull all my hair out. He dragged me through the kitchen and into the lounge, all the while shouting what a problem I was and how nobody wanted me. He hauled me into the bathroom and pulled me to my feet. I remember thinking I didn't need a bath. But he wasn't bathing me because I still had my clothes on. He lifted me up by my hair and the back of my jeans and tipped me upside down.

'See if you fuckin' like this!' he screamed.'

And before I could say another word, he slammed my head into the bathwater. I couldn't breathe. I closed my eyes at first but the panic of not being able to breathe made me open them again. I tried to scream but the water rushed into my mouth and into my lungs and I began to choke and splutter. It was the worst feeling in the world. My dad lifted my head out of the water, and I gagged. My stomach went into spasms and I vomited a horrid brown liquid into the bath.

It didn't stop him. 'You filthy little bitch!'

Before I could beg for mercy my head was back under water and I was swallowing my own vomit mixed in with the cold water. I clawed at his hands, but it was no use, he was in total control and I was completely helpless. Just when I thought I would drown; he pulled my head out of the water. He kept doing this until I eventually stopped fighting. When he was finished with me, he threw me in the corner of the bathroom with a towel and told me to clean myself up. I sat there crying for hours until I eventually ran some water and washed the vomit from my hair. When I walked back into the lounge Dad was reading a book.

He looked up. 'Let that be a lesson to you, next time I'll fucking leave you under the water and kill you.'

Dad gave me the head under the bathwater treatment about once a week. I learned quickly not to panic. I learned to hold my breath longer and longer each time because if I panicked and screamed and kicked and punched it would just be worse, because then he would beat me afterwards. He threatened to kill me each time he dragged me towards the bathroom but I sensed he didn't want to kill me, not really.

Dad began taking an interest in my homework and he was very strict. Woe betide me if I got a sum wrong or made a spelling mistake. He had a whiteboard in the lounge and would school me like a teacher. I started to dread it when he sat me in front of that whiteboard because I could answer seven or eight question in a row correctly, but if I had one wrong, I got a beating.

Dad was punching and kicking me more regularly now and over time I learned to cope with that as well. It was my normal daily life and I suppose I thought this was how all little girls were treated by their dads. Dad started making me wear strange clothes. They were very revealing and definitely not something a six-year-old should be wearing. He would make me walk around the flat with next to nothing on as he stared at me and one day he told me to remove my knickers. He told me I didn't need to wear them in the house. My sister started to visit us at the new house and stayed overnight a few times. We slept in the bedroom together while dad slept on the sofa and I somehow felt safer when she was there. It wasn't to last though; things were about to turn a lot more sinister.

Dad woke me up one day. I was fast asleep at the time and looked over at Chloe.

'Get up,' he whispered.

'Where are we going,' I asked.

'Just you,' he said, 'just me and you.'

He led me through to the lounge and told me to take off my nightie. I knew better than to disobey him and did as I was told.

'Lie on the floor.'

'But it's cold.'

'Lie on the fucking floor like I said.'

I lay on the floor and Dad took off his pyjamas. He was naked. I had never seen him like that before and it looked all weird. He lay down on top of me. He was heavy and breathing hard and he was touching me down there.

'Stop it Daddy, I don't like it.'

He was pushing something between my legs and forcing them apart. I screamed and he put his hand over my mouth. And then he pushed hard and the most agonising pain shot through me. I thought I was going to die and still he didn't stop and he kept pushing until eventually it was all over. I was sobbing by now. He climbed off me and walked out of the room, leaving me lying in the dark. I didn't know what had happened and it felt like the end of the world.

I lay in the dark for a long time and the bottom half of my body was on fire. My legs were burning and inside it felt like I had been stabbed by red hot daggers. It was hours before I dared to stand up and when I did I walked over and switched on the light. My legs were covered in blood and now I was convinced I was going to die. As I walked back to my room, I could hear him snoring quietly on the sofa. Why had he hurt me like this? I just couldn't understand it. I went to the bathroom and pulled some tissues out of a box and wiped myself down and then I went back to be and crawled in beside Chloe. She never stirred.

My worst nightmare had begun because if I thought that the attack would be the first and the last, I was sadly mistaken. Dad woke me again in the middle of the night two days later. This time Chloe had gone back to Mom's.

He sent me for a glass of water and when I returned from the kitchen, he threw it all over me.

'You've been calling for Mom in your sleep.'

'Have I?'

'Yes, you fucking little bitch, get your clothes off,' he said, 'and lie on the floor.'

I tried to run from the room, but he caught me by the hair and dragged me back through to the bedroom. Even at six years old I knew that if something hurt me this bad then it had to be wrong. I tried to scream again but it didn't stop him, he simply clasped his hand over my mouth.

'Shut the fuck up.'

I bit him and he squealed and punched me in the face.

'You fucking little bitch!'

He hit me so hard that the room started to spin and that made it easier, because I was floating in and out of consciousness. He was on top of me again and then it was all over. More blood, more tissues.

I was sobbing uncontrollably when I went to bed that night and he must have heard me, because he came into my room and sat on my bed.

'Stop complaining,' he said, 'it's a father's job to do this to his daughter.

Before he left the room he told me that there was no point in staying in my own bed and from tomorrow I would be sharing his bed.

11

Someone Please Help Me

We moved again, this time to a two-bedroom council house. Dad raped me most days and sometimes two or three times a day. He sometimes he woke me up in the middle of the night and raped me again. If I fought him or complained, he beat so I stopped fighting and I stopped complaining. Even so, he still found excuse to beat me. The slaps were a distant memory now because they had been replaced with kicks and punches and I regularly had black eyes now. When they asked me at school how I had got them I gave the excuse my dad told me to give. I'd fallen down the stairs, tripped over a dog or walked into a door. Looking back now I wonder what the hell the teachers were playing at. It was obvious to a blind man that I was having the shit beaten out of me so why didn't anybody do anything to help me?

Somebody must have reported that something was

going on behind the closed doors of 77 Tennessee Road, because now we had regular visits from Social Services. We always knew when they were coming and Dad would tidy the house, wash and put the dishes away and always make sure my bed had clean sheets even though I wasn't sleeping in it anymore.

He told me what to say to the social workers: everything is great, Dad is great, he's a caring father and I'm his little princess. He made sure that I would tell them I loved my bedroom and playing with my toys and playing games with the other kids in the street. He made me lie my head off. And smile, don't forget to smile he'd tell me.

When my sister came to stay it was better. He would put on an act for her and he'd allow us to stay together in my room and sleep together in my bed. I loved when Chloe came to visit or at least I did at first. Even Chloe's visits didn't stop him from raping me, he just waited until she was fast asleep. Dad would tip-toe through in the middle of the night and carry me half asleep into his bed where he'd rape me and then carry me back through to my bedroom and lay me gently down next to Chloe. It was all so normal and life went on.

I was seven years old when Dad made me drink alcohol for the first time. Dad drank alcohol constantly, mostly Guinness or white wine. I hated the taste of Guinness the first time he forced me to drink it, making it clear that I would be in for a good beating if I refused.

'It's awful, Dad.'

'Drink it up, the whole glass.'

It was a half pint glass and he made me drink all of

it. I immediately vomited it all up and he howled with laughter before slapping me and telling me to clean it up. By the time I'd cleaned it up there was another half pint glass on the table and he forced me to drink that one as well. It wasn't so bad second time around and I managed to keep it down.

He made me drink wine until I saw double and again, he would burst out laughing. Then he would throw me on the floor and rape me. He introduced me to spirits like Malibu and Aftershock. I think he thought it was easier to rape me when I was drunk - perhaps I didn't struggle so much. Other times he didn't seem to care.

And after a while I thought why not? It was OK to drink, because I would hardly feel the pain of what he did. Sometimes I would black out completely and that was best of all.

He would come in from work and simply say, 'Okay, into the lounge and get your clothes off, this is what's going to happen.'

He was drinking a lot now. We'd sometimes go over to visit my aunties and they'd also be drinking and smoking the funny cigarettes. Dad would always want sex after he had had a drink and I knew what was going to happen. Sometimes we'd leave my auntie's house well after midnight, even on school nights. It was a thirty-minute walk home and there was never any money for taxis no matter how bad the weather. Dad would pull me down a dark alley and have sex with me and I was always terrified that someone would see us. It was in one of those alleys that he made me perform oral sex on him the first time.

He made me squat down in front of him and I can remember being relieved that he hadn't pushed me against a wall to have sex. I didn't know what he was doing or what he wanted me to do but I soon found out. Sometimes when he was drunk, he'd rape me on a bench in a public park. Even when it was cold and raining, he didn't seem to care. That's a heavily populated part of Derby and it's a miracle that he was never caught.

Dad was into kick boxing and weightlifting and he got me involved at well, whether I wanted to or not. He also enrolled me in a gymnastics class, and he was a tough taskmaster who was obsessed with practice. He made me practice every spare moment I had and sometimes he'd sit and watch me while he was drinking beer. One day he got angry with me for not putting a hundred percent into my training.

'Right that's it, you can stop. Get me another beer.'

I walked through to the fridge in the kitchen where he kept the beer. When I returned to the lounge, I was aware of something flying towards me and an empty beer bottle hit me on the side of my head and smashed to pieces. The neck of the broken bottle ripped into the skin behind my ear and as the blood started pouring out of my head I fainted. We went to hospital on the bus. I was in terrible pain and Dad held a tea towel on my head to try and stop the blood. I was lapsing in and out of consciousness and eventually I passed out and woke up and when I woke up I was in hospital. Whenever dad took me to hospital or to the doctor, I knew that my injuries were bad. The nursing staff were very suspicious, because there was blood all over me and my hair was matted with it.

A nice middle-aged nurse sat holding my hand. 'How did this happen love?' she asked.
Dad was on the other side of the treatment table and without hesitation he answered for me and said I had been practicing my gymnastics and I crashed into a coffee table. The nurse looked direct into my eyes.
'Is that right?' she asked.
Dad was glaring at me and I had no choice. 'Yes,' I said.
They glued my head back together and Dad sent me to school the very next day. Only one teacher asked what had happened.
'I was practicing my gymnastics,' I said, 'and I fell onto the coffee table.'
She knew, the nurse knew, my Mom, my aunties and uncles, Nan and Granddad, Social Services and the Police all knew what my father was doing to me but no one lifted a finger to help me. Nobody did anything. They let me down, everybody let me down.
I found out many years later that the school had reported my bruises and scratches and my black eyes to Social Services and it had all been logged, but nobody did a thing about it.

They say violence breeds violence and how right they are. I was absolutely controlled and dominated at home where I had no choice but there was no way was I going to be intimidated or bullied at school. I was quite small and lived with my father and everyone knew about my dysfunctional family and that my mother didn't want me. I was just the sort of person the bullies homed in on and they tortured me. I was eight or nine years old when I had my first fight at school. Sam* had been goading me for a while; calling me names and telling me that her friends, who were all much older than me, were going to beat me up after school. She threatened me with violence for a few days but nothing happened so I started to think it was all hot air and told myself I could cope with it. But it got progressively worse. She would deliberately bump into me in the school corridors or give me an odd slap when nobody was looking. One evening when I was leaving school she pushed me in the chest.

'Any day now Bitch and you're going to get it. We're all ready and waiting.'

I now knew she meant it. It was going to happen sooner or later, and I began to get quite worried. I decided there was only one course of action - the next time she laid a finger on me I would retaliate. Two days later the school bell rang and I walked towards the gates to where Dad always picked me up and Sam was waiting for me with her older friends. They were laughing and hurling insults at me and I went to walk around them, but Sam blocked my path.

She pushed me in the chest. 'Come on little girl, stick up for yourself.'

She didn't know what hit her. My kick boxing training stepped in and I took a step forward and jabbed my left hand into the centre of her nose, following it up with a right hook to the chin. She crumpled like a pack of cards, holding her nose and squealing as the blood ran between her fingers. Before I knew it, I was being restrained by her friends and a couple of teachers sprinted out from the school building. A couple of days later the school told me I was being excluded for the rest of the week. Sam could stay in school and the feeling of injustice was indescribable. For once, Dad was on my side as I explained what had happened. He told me that I always had to stand up for myself.

'If they hit you hard, hit them back twice as hard,' he said.

I returned to school the following week and people were staying out of my way. I had acquired a reputation among my peers, but unfortunately also with the headmaster and teachers and they were all watching me closely.

A week later one of Sam's friends challenged me in the playground. He surrounded me with a group of his friends and said he was going to teach me a lesson for what I had done to his friend. I told him I didn't want to fight and tried to walk away but he wouldn't listen. He pushed me a few times and then slapped me hard across the face. I saw red and kicked him as hard as I could in the crotch. While he groaned and bent forward, I threw a combination of three or four punches to his head and face and it was all over. I left him in a heap on the wet concrete and turned to walk away as his mates looked on helplessly. Halfway across the school yard one of the teachers caught up with me and I was hauled in front of the head. Once again I hadn't started the fight but because I'd finished it and won, the punishment was handed down to me. I pleaded with the head that I hadn't started it and explained how I had tried to get out of the circle and run away and had only retaliated when the boy slapped me. The Head listened, wrote something in a note pad and then gave me his decision. I was to be permanently

excluded.
This time Dad was livid.
Our house was close to the school and he knew Sam walked past our window every night.
Dad said she was to blame and ordered me to beat her up in order to teach her a lesson. I said no, but Dad punched me and said if I didn't beat her up, he would give me the biggest hiding I had ever experienced. I had no choice. And so, two days later, just at the time the school bell rang for the end of the day we both stared out of the window looking for Sam. I spotted her when she was about fifty yards from the house and went out to confront her. I stood in front of her as she walked towards me and I could see the fear on her face and I felt sorry for her. I didn't want to hit her, and I looked back at Dad's face in the window. He raised his hand and clenched it into a fist and I knew exactly what that meant. I punched her in the face and then the stomach. She burst into tears and before I had a chance to hit her again her friends piled onto me. I threw a few punches and someone had me by the hair but Dad ran out of the house and broke it up. This time Dad and I were both called into school and Dad went so berserk in the head's office that he threatened to call the police.
A new social worker visited us around that time. This confirms to me that the authorities knew something was going on but they did nothing about it. The girl who came to our house was small and timid, less than five-foot-tall and she was clearly intimidated by my dad.
He opened the door to her for the first time. 'Who are you, what the fuck do you want?'

I heard him swearing at her. I poked my head around the door and saw her standing on the step, looking terrified. Why on earth had Social Services sent the weakest looking social worker they could find?

'You're not stepping a fucking foot in my house now fuck off before I lose my temper.'

The poor girl was visibly shaking with fear but insisted she had some sort of court order that allowed her into the house.

'Fuck off you little bitch!' Dad screamed at her.

Although the girl looked terrified, she would not be moved. 'You either allow me in Mr Clifton or I'll be back in an hour with the police and they will force entry and you will be arrested.'

I admired her resolve and courage. Dad must have realised that she was wasn't going anywhere and asked her to give him a minute. He closed the door and came looking for me. He sat me down, told me that I needed to cover a bruise on my face and that if I told the social worker anything that he had been doing to me he would break the girl's neck. Dad ran quickly upstairs and I heard him moving about in my bedroom. He returned to the front door, opened it and she walked in. She started by asking to see me alone.

'That's not going to happen,' my Dad said, 'she's my daughter, not yours.'

She looked at me and I covered my bruise with my fringe as dad had instructed.

She wandered around the house while Dad followed her.

'I need to see Shannon's bedroom,' she asked.

I didn't think anything of this request at the time, but

I do remember a few other social workers asking the same question. Could it be that even then they suspected that sexual abuse was taking place? She walked up the stairs and Dad followed her. I crept up the stairs behind them. I couldn't understand why she wanted to see my bedroom, because I hadn't slept in there for some months. When I peered into my room and looked at my bed the cover had been pulled back and the pillows were scattered around. Dad had made the bed look as if it had been slept in. Then the penny dropped. I was eight years old and the penny finally dropped. Social Services knew what was going on and that's why they had sent a social worker; that's why they were looking into a little girl's room - to see if everything looked normal. I have a vague recollection that the police also came to inspect my bedroom at one point, but nobody did anything and nothing changed. We went back downstairs and she sat me down in the lounge with my father. She asked me question after question and I gave all the answers I knew Dad wanted to give. I was a good girl; my education was going well and so were the gymnastic classes. I loved living with just my dad, he was kind and considerate and I was his little princess.

The girl took some notes and when she was finished she stood up. 'I must get going, I've another appointment in town.'

Dad was smiling at her now and the initial threats and intimidation had been long forgotten.

'Is everything okay love?'

'Yes, everything is fine Mr Clifton.'

A week later he raped me outside the back door in

our garden. He had been angry all day and I knew something was going to happen. He held his hand over my mouth to stop me screaming and I couldn't believe he was taking the chance with the neighbour's fence only a few yards away. I crawled up the stairs and went to bed crying but after ten minutes he came to bed and it started all over again and he raped me repeatedly throughout that night. I was in so much pain, I felt as if someone had ripped out my soul and stamped all over it.

A short while later, I was reading a book in my bedroom when Dad called me through to the lounge.

'There's something I want you to watch?' he asked.

He had a strange look on his face and he was smiling. I noticed the green light on the DVD player was on.

'Are we going to watch a movie?' I asked.

'Yes,' he said, 'come and sit next to me.'

When I sat down he pressed play and I watched the screen.

The movie started normally - a man knocking on a front door and then a blond lady answered and asked him inside. It wasn't like any movie I had seen before and I began to get a weird feeling about it. My father was introducing me to my first porn movie. I was eight years old.

The action moved on quite quickly and the lady started to perform oral sex on the man. I recognised it because it was exactly what my father made me do to him. I closed my eyes, but my father must have looked at me because he slapped me hard across the head.

'Fucking watch it.'

He forced me to watch it for over an hour. At first the

couple were having sex but then the movie moved on and more people joined the scene and they brought a young girl into the room. She was tied up and some men were treating her badly; they were hitting her with whips, and she had something in her mouth which stopped her from crying out. Dad told me that we had to copy everything they were doing and by now I was shaking with fear. The horrible things my father was doing to me was about to be stepped up to another level. After the movie had finished my Dad told me to undress and he left the room. A couple of minutes later he returned with some rope.

The pornography evenings would be a regular occurrence for the next few years.

12

Expelled and Thrown into The Lion's Den

I was nine years old when I had my first sex education lesson at school. The girls and boys were split up and the girls taught by a female teacher and the boys by a male teacher.

We walked into the classroom and all the girls were giggling. The teacher made us sit on the carpet in a big semi-circle and started off showing us diagrams of boys' and girls' private parts and gave them their proper names. She started to describe the vagina and told us how it had an opening where the male penis could enter and the act of sex could take place. She told us about ejaculation and sperm and fertilization. Nine months later a baby is born she announced casually. A shiver ran the length of my spine. What? Surely, she was wrong. By now my Dad had been having sex with me for three years and another family member before that. I hadn't had any babies. She brought up a photograph of a pregnant woman with a huge stomach and I breathed a sigh of relief because my stomach was as flat as a pancake. She is lying, I thought to myself, sex doesn't make babies. The lesson dragged on. Five minutes before the end of the lesson she became very serious and told us how no one should touch our private parts until we were at least sixteen and only with our consent.

'You can touch yourself,' she said matter of factly. 'It's called masturbation and doesn't cause any harm but on no account should any man touch you there or penetrate you with his penis.'

I was speechless. I started to tremble.

'The man can go to prison,' she said.

I left the class almost in tears, but I held myself together. What was my father doing to me? He said it was normal and that all fathers did that to their daughters. That started me thinking. If that's what fathers did to their daughters, then why tell me it always had to be kept a secret? He told me a hundred times not to tell anyone. That's when I understood that what my father was doing to me was wrong, it was against the law and he could go to prison.

And yet, as I walked out of school that evening a part of me didn't trust the teacher. What if she was lying? She had lied about pregnancy and babies so perhaps she was lying about that. I wanted to talk to somebody about what was happening to me but there was nobody.

Two days later I punched one of the older boys in the face because he called me ugly. It didn't particularly upset me as it wasn't the worst name anyone had called me, but I overreacted and lost my temper. I was in the headmaster's office again and a day later Dad was called into the school. They said I would be excluded permanently; I was consistently breaching the school's behaviour policy and it was seriously harming the welfare of the other pupils. They told dad that we would have to apply for an alternative school.

'Over my fucking dead body,' Dad ranted at the head, 'those fucking schools are full of assholes.'

'Please moderate your language Mr. Clifton.'

Dad stood and leaned over the desk. I swear he was about to hit the headmaster, who leaned away from him and threatened to call the police.

'Fuck you and fuck your school,' he said, and we left.

When we got home, Dad told me to take off my clothes. He removed his belt and beat me mercilessly while I begged him to stop. Then he raped me. Dad was as true as his word. He wouldn't send me to the alternative school, and he said he would home school me. It wouldn't be difficult he said and phoned the school to tell them of his decision. Dad was a labourer at that time and he left home at seven in the morning and returned around six in the evening. I wondered how he was going to do it. Two days later he handed me a pile of books. 'Read these,' he said, 'I'm going to be testing you on them.'

Every few days Dad would sit me in front of the white board and test me. My tests always resulted in a beating or a rape and often, both.

I was 'home schooled' for over a year before the authorities stepped in and said I was going to Laudau Forte Secondary School. Dad wasn't pleased but he knew he had no option. He was worried that I would start talking to people about what was going on and before I left for school every day he reminded me about 'our secret' and told me what the consequences would be if I let anything slip. He said he would kill me. I met new friends at school and it was nice because I hadn't mixed with anyone my own age for over twelve months, because Dad wouldn't allow me out of the house without him. He was paranoid about me talking to people. Dad would always drop me at school and made sure he was there to collect me. I learned to stay away from boys because if he ever saw me walking out of school with a boy, he would start calling me names and accuse me of flirting with them as soon as I got into the car. It was now clear to me at ten years old that my father thought he owned me. I was his wife. I took care of him, cooked and cleaned for him and was the outlet for any form of sexual release he demanded. I told the boys at school not to talk to me. It was better that way.

By now we all had Facebook at school. Dad set my account up and he created the email account and password. At the time I thought he was being reasonable for once, but I now know he was spying on me by reading all the posts and studying every photo in detail. He knew everything there was to know about all my Facebook friends and I made sure that all my friends were girls. If I did get a request from a boy I declined and deleted them. We had a group of about six friends on there and we chatted about everything and nothing. One of my friends mentioned a boy called Lucas* and asked why I wouldn't go out with him. I said I didn't know anyone by that name, and she replied, 'Well he knows you and he really fancies you. You should go out with him.'

I heard dad stomping down the stairs so I closed off the computer screen in case he saw it and picked up a book and tried to act innocent. We ate some supper and afterwards I started to wash the dishes. As I placed the last cup onto the draining board Dad spun me around violently.

'Who the fuck is Lucas you, little whore?'

I panicked and I could hardly breathe. 'I don't know Dad.'

'Fucking liar.'

He drew back his fist. 'I'll ask you again, who the fuck is Lucas?'

'I don't know.'

I sank to my knees. I knew what was coming and I couldn't take much more. His fist propelled towards me and there was an almighty crash. I waited for the blow, for the pain, for the blood. But there wasn't any. I glanced to my side. There was a huge hole in the cupboard door.

'Who is Lucas?'

'A boy at school but I don't know him, I have never spoken to him.'

He smashed another hole in the other side of the cupboard. In a way it was worse than getting hit. Dad did that a lot - play the psychological game and threaten me with violence. He didn't only threaten me with physical but with sexual violence as well. Dad had recently started to rape me anally. That night, he was especially rough and it was very painful. When he was finished with me, I lay on the floor sobbing for ages, begging him never to do it again.

'Who the fuck is he?'

'I don't know Dad, I swear.'

As I cowered by the cupboard door, he threatened me with more anal sex.

Dad's interrogation went on for a long time that night. At one point I wet myself and he went mad. He punched several more holes in the cupboard and eventually he punched me as well when there was no cupboard door left. He punched me just once and the lights went out as I slumped to the floor. It was dark by the time I regained consciousness and I was lying in a pool of blood and my own freezing cold urine. I made my way groggily upstairs and into the bathroom to clean myself up. That was the night I also started my period.

13

My Father, the Psychopath

I had always been skinny and fit, because Dad made sure that I trained hard with weights and would often wake me at four thirty in the morning to go on a five-mile run with him.

Now and then as we ran through the dark streets of Derby, we would pass a police car on patrol and Dad would wave and the policemen would wave back. To this day I wonder why no policemen ever stopped us and asked what the hell was going on - a ten-year-old girl running with a man at that time of the morning. Not once did a policeman ever stop us.

One day Dad told me we were going shopping. He had a strange smile on his face and took me into town on the bus. He made me wait across the road from a shop that had blacked out windows and was called Simply Pleasure. I had no idea what sort of shop it was, but he told me with a grin that he was going to buy me some presents.

When he came out of the shop, I asked him if I could see the presents.

'Not here,' he said, 'wait until we get home.'

I day or two later he walked into the lounge and said it was time to see my toys. That's how he described them. I will never forget the day he walked in with that terrible box.

'I have some toys, Shannon, we are going to play with some toys.'

He sat me down on the sofa and for once he looked happy, but I studied his face and I knew something was very wrong. He opened the box and lifted something up in front of me. I had never seen anything like it before.

'Get your clothes off,' he ordered.

Over the next two hours he subjected me to a horrific, painful ordeal as he raped me with a selection of sex toys. He raped me vaginally and anally. When I complained he beat me and then it started all over again. I thought it would never end and only when I lapsed into unconsciousness after another beating did he leave me alone. When I came around, he was gone. The toys had been packed away and the box was gone. He had left a note to say that he had gone to work.

My dad would drive me to random places and rape me in fields and forests. Sometimes he would park the car, order me into the back seat and rape me there. Sometimes he couldn't be bothered to climb into the back seat and he would force me to perform oral sex on him. The sexual side of his treatment was getting worse and every day there seemed to be something more sinister going on in his head. It was as if he was trying to think up more warped things he could do to me, he was always looking for something else, always experimenting with me. He would try anything. He filmed me with his phone or tablet and he sometimes took photos with the timer. We would drive out to deserted forest car parks in the Peak District and he'd make me take my clothes off and photograph or video me doing sexual poses. He took a lot of photos and videos of that and dozens of videos of me performing oral sex on him while he held the camera. Other times he positioned the tablet in the lounge and filmed himself having sex with me and other times he tied me up, had sex with me and beat me while he filmed it. He took pleasure from seeing me suffer and he enjoyed it when I was crying or screaming or begging him to stop while I was tied up. I didn't know it at the time, but as I sit and write this chapter I'm convinced that my father is a psychopath. Psychopaths don't have that inner voice that tells us that what we're doing is wrong, they don't have any conscience and they can't feel empathy. Empathy is when you or I can place ourselves in another person's shoes and understand how they're feeling. If my father had any conscience or if he was able to feel an ounce of empathy for me, he would not have done any of these things to me. This surely explains why my father beat me, stabbed me, threw bottles and chairs at me and flung me round the room like a doll with not a word of remorse or regret.

Psychopaths are also outstanding liars and my father fooled everyone; he made them all believe he was a fabulous father who would do anything for his

daughter and sometimes even managed to convince himself. He brainwashed everyone, even me and despite everything he put me through I still loved him. In my opinion, the worst kind of psychopath is the one who takes great enjoyment from the pain and distress he causes his victim.
Psychopaths like my father.

In spite of my strict training regime I noticed that I had begun to put on a little weight and that my stomach was hard. At first, I put it down to puberty - we had been learning about it at school. I started thinking about what the sex education teacher had said about pregnancy and the nine-month cycle. Don't be silly, I told myself. I had just turned eleven, girls of eleven didn't have babies.
My stomach was getting bigger, my body was changing, I had missed my period for a few months and my stomach. Despite wearing baggy tops and loose-fitting trousers I could not live in denial any longer. I couldn't tell my friends or my teachers and I had no one else to turn to. After four months it was obvious to me that I was pregnant and I studied my body every night before I went to bed. At five months I decided I had to tell someone. How Dad hadn't noticed I'll never know, and it took me another full month before I finally plucked up the courage to tell him. That evening, Dad called to say he would be thirty home in minutes and to make sure his dinner was on the table.
As he sat on the sofa eating his dinner, I came out with it.
'Dad, I think I might be pregnant.'
He looked up. 'You're eleven, you can't be pregnant.'

I lifted up my baggy t-shirt and showed him my stomach. The colour drained from his face as his jaw nearly hit the floor. How would he respond, I thought? He responded by standing up and throwing a wooden foot stool at me. It hit me in the chest with such force that it knocked me over. He ran over and started to kick and stamp on me. This time my face and head were safe, because he was directing every blow at my stomach.

The pain was indescribable and I struggled for breath. I thought he was going to kill me.

'Stop!' I shouted. 'Stop!'

He continued kicking me in the stomach and he picked me up a few times and threw me across the room like a ragdoll. He beat me until he was exhausted and collapsed out of breath on the floor. A few minutes later he got up and it started all over again. There was no end to it and I was convinced he was busy killing me. He kicked and kicked and kicked; sometimes he flipped me over and beat me on the back, then turn me over and have another go on my stomach. He lifted me by the hair and forced my back against the wall and then he punched me in the stomach over and over again until my legs turned to jelly and I collapsed onto the carpet. The last thing I can remember was being dragged up the stairs by the hair. This was it; he was dragging me upstairs to kill me.

*

I woke up in bed and I instinctively knew that there was no baby inside me anymore. I lifted the covers and looked down. My stomach was black and between my legs was a pool of dried blood. Then the pain registered and I screamed. My thighs were black and blue and as I started to cry it was as if someone was plunging a dagger into my ribs.

Dad walked into the bedroom. He sat on the bed. 'You've been sleeping for two days.'

'Where's the baby?' I asked.

'I've taken care of it,' he said, 'your dad will always take care of things.'

I tried to speak again but my body was wracked with pain. I tried to lift my head, but it wouldn't move. I tried to move my legs and fee, but they wouldn't move. I tried to wiggle my fingers. Nothing. I lay in bed for a week convinced that my father had paralysed me but gradually the feeling started to come back in my arms and legs. I wish it hadn't, because every time I woke up another part of my body hurt like hell. I lived on Paracetamol to dull the pain. When I did eventually get out of bed and stood up I left a pool of blood. I had never felt such pain and I can't begin to describe the emotional turmoil of realising that my unborn baby had literally been kicked out of me. I bled for many days, but I can't remember exactly how many. Perhaps nine or ten. After I stopped bleeding Dad sent me back to school. At this point Dad wasn't at home very often. He was working nightshift at Tesco and doing a college course during the day and we were like passing ships. That suited me fine. I cooked his dinner and washed the dishes and cleaned up afterwards. Perhaps the violence and sexual abuse was over, I thought. Perhaps the death of my child had at least done some good. I dared to dream. I did a Google search to see how big a six-month-old foetus is. It's

twelve inches long and weighs two pounds. I recoiled in horror. Where had the baby gone? It wouldn't just fall out of me! What had my father done to me? Where had he put my dead child, had he buried it in the garden or put it out with the rubbish? Or had he had just thrown it into the river?
I cried myself to sleep that night. I had been emotionally attached to my little baby and my dad had gone and killed it. The emotional pain was much worse than the physical pain and I have never recovered from it. My dad murdered my baby by kicking me in the stomach so violently that I had a miscarriage.

I was back at school and I wandered from one class to the next like a zombie. I had lost the will to live. I felt like shit and I knew I looked like shit, because my friends all commented that I looked like shit. I expected to be called to the school nurse or the welfare officer, but nobody ever questioned me. I sought solace in the school library and read anything I could get a hold of. I tried to escape and immerse myself in the Harry Potter books. It was wonderful escapist fantasy and I read voraciously to take away the pain and to somehow transport myself to another dimension. I had an overwhelming desire to tell someone what I had been through and I started to look at the class teachers, my form teachers, the deputy head and even the school nurse. Why did none of them register the pain in my eyes?

Please help me, someone please talk to me.

Oh, they knew alright. They knew because I could see how they all looked at me. They stared. Everybody stared at me, but nobody lifted a finger. None of them filled me with any confidence, any flicker of hope. I convinced myself that nobody would believe me and because Dad had disposed of the body there wasn't a shred of evidence.

I had formed a friendship with a black girl called Tania*. I had begun to confide in her about the violence Dad was subjecting me to but couldn't bring myself to tell her about the sexual abuse or that he had murdered my unborn child. We became quite close and I trusted her, but Dad suspected this and warned me to stay away from her. He beat me up one night.

'Stay away from that black bastard,' he threatened, 'let that be a warning to you.'

I almost laughed at him. Dad never needed any excuse to beat me up so this was hardly a threat.

14

I Want to Die

Dad had been threatening to kill me for years. While it frightened me I never really believed that he actually would murder me and yet the fact that he had deliberately murdered my baby by kicking it out of me made me wonder whether he was capable of killing me too. Exactly three months after my miscarriage Dad one day described in great detail how he would kill me and how he would dispose of my body.

The school had organised a summer camp - I think it was somewhere in the Peak District National Park – and for some reason they insisted I go. Dad was furious and fought the school tooth and nail. They asked him what the reason was I couldn't attend and asked him to write a letter. Of course, there was no reason and although Dad wrote something about a non-existent medical condition, the school checked my attendance record, spoke to the school nurse and said there was no reason why I couldn't attend. They said if Dad kept me away he would be reported to the local authority. And so Dad allowed me to go. It was the greatest three days of my life.

We slept in big dormitories and on the last night we slept in a tent. I had never slept in a tent and before we fell asleep, we all lay in our sleeping bags looking up at the night sky discussing how big the universe was. I was at peace with the world, because there were no beatings and I wasn't woken in the middle of the night to be raped. For the first time in a good long while I wasn't scared of my own shadow. Only when I was completely exhausted and I could hardly lift my head did I crawl into my tent and fall asleep. I slept like a baby.

At lunchtime we left and I sat with my head against the window and cried. I wanted to live there forever because I knew that within a few hours I would be back in hell. I couldn't have imagined however, how bad hell was going to be. Dad was waiting in the car as the bus pulled up outside the school gates. I climbed from the coach and got my bag from the luggage compartment below. As soon as I saw Dad's face, I knew I was in trouble. What had I done I asked myself? I hadn't been naughty and the teachers wouldn't have called him. As I walked towards the car I wondered if there had been some sort of accident. Had my brother or sister been hurt or had someone died?

'Hi Dad.'

'Don't fucking hi Dad me, why haven't you been answering my texts?'

'I have dad, I answered your texts.'

'Not fucking all of them.'

The girls had said that the reception in the Peak District is very poor; something to do with all the hills. Perhaps I had missed some of his texts.

I took the phone from my pocket. 'The reception was poor Dad, perhaps I missed some.'

'You missed a fucking dozen; I was worried sick.' He lunged at me. 'Give me the fucking phone.'

He threw it onto the ground and stamped on it, smashing it to pieces.

'You're fucking taking the piss, you bitch.'

I shook my head. 'No, Dad, no.'

He opened the door and pushed me in as he walked around to the driver's side. He started the engine and the tyres squealed as we pulled away from the school.

He started verbally abusing me before he had even turned the corner.

'I know why you didn't message me you fucking little whore. You've been fucking the boys.'

'No Dad.'

'You've been fucking them in your little tents while the teachers have been out on the piss.'

'No Dad, we slept in different dormitories, there were no boys anywhere near us.'

'Don't you fucking lie to me.'

He brought the car to a sharp stop and if I hadn't been wearing my seatbelt I would have flown through the window.

He unbuckled his belt and turned to face me. 'You're going to end up like that fucking phone.'

Before I had a chance to answer him his fist smashed into my nose. There was a crack and a loud popping noise and the searing pain shot through my head. I struggled to breathe and I noticed a splash of blood on the windscreen and suddenly there was blood everywhere. I looked down. My white school blouse was red; there wasn't a white patch to be seen.

Dad buckled his belt up and drove off while the tears rolled down my face and mixed with the blood. During the short journey home Dad described what he was going to do to me.

'I'm going to kill you, you fucking slag.'

I whimpered like a beaten dog. 'Please Dad, nothing happened.'

'I have the ironing board set up at home and first I'm going to burn your fucking face off. Then I´ll get the hammer and I'm going to smash every fucking bone in that slag body of yours.'

Dad was smiling while he told me exactly what he was going to do and how he was going to cut up my body and bury it under the paving stones in the garden. He had it all planned. When we arrived home, he ran to my side of the car. I was too scared to move and he leaned over and unbuckled my seatbelt, grabbed me by the hair and dragged me into the house. He took me straight into the lounge and pointed to where, sure enough, the ironing board was standing upright in the corner. He pointed at the coffee table where the iron and a large hammer were on display.

'You thought I was joking, didn't you?'

I shook my head. I tried to speak, but my whole body was frozen in fear; my throat and lips dry. I couldn't speak and I couldn't beg for my life.

Before I knew what was happening, he lifted me up and carried me towards the ironing board. I struggled a bit.

'Stay fucking still or you'll regret it.'
I was convinced he was going to kill me and I did as he said so that I could get it over with as quick as possible. What did I have to live for anyway?
While he was lifting me onto the ironing board, I lost control of my bladder.
'You dirty fucking bitch!'

He left me on the ironing board and plugged in the iron. I lay there petrified while he waited for the iron to heat up. I was shaking like a rag doll; I was still covered in blood and I was lying in my own urine. We waited. Dad flicked the face of the iron with the tip of his finger and spat on it. The saliva sizzled and rolled to the floor. Then he picked up the iron, walked over to me and held it just an inch or two above my face. I could feel the heat. He held it there for some time while I begged for my life. He plunged it down several times, just missing my face. He was enjoying his game and although he never did burn me or hit me with the hammer, for nearly an hour I was convinced I was going to die a horrible death.
Eventually he had had his fun and pulled me onto the floor, ripped off my bloodstained blouse and my knickers and raped me. He beat me up and raped me all weekend. It was the worst weekend of my life. The violence was constant and he was more sadistic than he had ever been in the past. My whole body ached; especially my thighs, my ribs and my back. I could hardly stand up straight and just the effort of walking sent my body into spasms of agony. Every time I touched my nose, pain ripped through my head and a nauseous feeling washed over me. My nose was broken, and I told dad I needed to go to the

hospital. He told me to stop complaining and said I was a drama queen.

I drank Paracetamol for breakfast, lunch and supper. He sent me to school on the Monday and I looked like a panda. He must have felt sure that he wouldn't be found out by the authorities, because no one had accused him of mistreating me in the past so why should they start now?

He was right. Nobody said a word, and no one questioned why I looked like I had gone ten rounds with a heavyweight boxer. Later that week my mum saw me in town and noticed what a mess I was. My eyes were puffed up now, the bruises were turning a pale purple colour and there were scratches all over my face. I now realised that Mum was scared of Dad too but when he left, she told me she would tell my brother's social worker to look into my case. I had social workers visiting the house regularly and they must have known what was happening but they did nothing. I dared to hope that perhaps my brother's social worker would act.

15

Our Little Secret

I wondered if suicide was the answer. The following Monday I wandered around school aimlessly, spending most of my time in the school library. I skipped three or four lessons, because I didn't care anymore; I had lost the will to live. In the afternoon one of the teachers found me in the library and said it was time for our dance class. I broke down and I told her I wanted to see the school nurse. I'd had enough, I had to tell someone. I told her about my father punching my nose and I said I was in so much pain that I needed to go to hospital. She examined me and touched the bridge of my nose. I nearly hit the roof.

'Yes,' she said, 'it's a trip to the hospital for you, girl.'

One of the teachers took me to hospital in their car.

I was x-rayed and the doctor confirmed that my nose was broken. My dad arrived soon after because the school had phoned him. Dad was anxious and keen to get away as a couple of doctors fussed around me. 'Is this going to take long?' he asked more than once. I think they straightened it; I remember crying out in pain as one of the doctor's applied some pressure. A nurse was there and asked me how I had done it.

I glanced at Dad, then back to the nurse, 'I've been on a school camp, I hurt it there.'

'How?' she asked.

'We were wrestling.'

I started to cry when the nurse informed me that she would have to call Social Care but for once they weren't tears of pain, they were tears of relief. I returned to school the same day and sought sanctuary in the library again. One of the teachers came in and said the nurse had told her what had happened. She said they had called Dad and asked him to come to school and that he was on his way. Dad kicked off big time when he came to school. He was violent towards several teachers and stormed out of the meeting when they eventually called the police. Someone must have told him I was in the library because the silence was shattered as he kicked the door open and screamed at the top of his voice, 'Get your fucking arse over here now!'

The librarian sat shaking with fear and said nothing as he dragged me out by the arm. This is it, I thought. Now they know. Everybody knows; the teachers know; the nurse knows and so do Social Services and I have the broken nose to prove it.

Dad was furious in the car but he didn't hit me. He said that I'd 'blown it' and he'd had enough. He said I would be living with Mom from now on. Within half an hour four police vans drove into the street and pulled up outside the house. A dozen of the biggest policemen I'd ever seen piled into the front garden and Dad knew the game was up. While I expected a fight, Dad walked out of the house calmly and held out his hands while a policeman handcuffed him and put him in the back of the van.

A policewoman approached me. 'You can't stay here tonight darling, where can we take you?'

'My nan's house,' I said.

I told Nan and Granddad that Dad had attacked me and they just sat around the table shaking their heads, drinking cups of tea. At this point I still hadn't told anyone about the sexual abuse. I went to bed and cried for hours. I was still in agony with my nose and wondered when it would stop throbbing, but at least I was feeling peaceful and it felt good to have told someone at last. Perhaps it was all over.

They let Dad out the following morning and he turned up at Nan's while we were having breakfast. What was going on, why had they let him out, why hadn't he been sent to prison?

Dad was cool and calm, putting on a show for Nan and Grandad and said it was an accident and he had only meant to frighten me. They knew the truth, because I had told them. The police had told him not to come to Nan's house, but he came anyway, because Dad was invincible and untouchable and once again he had defied the authorities and the police and no one was there to stop him. I listened to my grandparents in amazement as the took my dad's side and told me that Dad hadn't meant to punch me and if I didn't tell the truth, he could go to prison for a long time.

'You have to tell them it was an accident,' Nan said, 'otherwise he'll be locked up again. Is that what you

want Shannon?'
Three adults against one little girl.
An hour or so later a police car pulled up outside the house and Dad ran out the back door. The police were with someone from Social Care and they wanted to speak to me on my own, but Nan wouldn't let them in. She said her two dogs were dangerous and that if the police set foot in the door, they would attack them. The policeman was shouting through the letter box that she needed to move the dogs into another room. It was nothing more than a delaying tactic while Nan took a hold of me and urged me to tell the police it was an accident. I nodded and she locked the dogs into a back bedroom and opened the front door. They sat with me for about twenty minutes and all the time I said that my injuries were the result of an accident. They didn't believe me; I could see in their eyes that they didn't believe me. In the end they gave up asking me.
After the police and Social Care left, Dad reappeared. He was different; it was now out in the open and he kept apologising to me, saying he didn't want me to have to live with my mom. He said I was his princess and he would always take care of me. He was so sorry he had hit me but it had been an accident.
What planet was he on, what was going through his head? I had relived every moment during the car journey during which he had punched me and I remembered exactly how he had threatened to smash me up like my phone. And when I'd got home, he'd threatened me with a hammer and a hot iron. How in God's name had any of that been by accident?
'If you don't want to live with Mom or get taken into care and be looked after by strangers then you will

have to tell them it was an accident.'

I didn't know what to say. I looked at Dad. His eyes were menacing and yet kind looking at the same time. I wondered if this could be a turning point. Now that everyone knew he had hit me then surely he could never hit me again.

'It was an accident,' he gushed with a sickly grin plastered all across his face, 'tell them it was an accident, Princess.'

I played back the incident in my mind. It was no accident; the scene was imprinted on my brain. My head hurt and I massaged my temples. I knew I hadn't imagined it and yet Dad seemed so convincing.

'I made a mistake Princess, I'm so sorry. Will you tell them it was an accident?'

'Yes, Daddy.'

And I did. The next day I went back to school and told them it was an accident. My father collected me from school that night and took me home. There was a social worker standing at the door waiting for us and Dad invited her in with a big smile and even made her a cup of tea. Dad told her all about 'the accident' and I confirmed everything he said and even apologised for wasting their time. I was lying, but surely the social worker and the teachers could see that I was lying? Days passed and nothing happened. Nan had said that I could go and live there if it ever happened again, but I didn't see her for weeks afterwards. I expected a knock on the door from Social Care or the police to turn up mob handed while they removed me from Dad's care but nothing happened. I told so many people that time, but they all let me down and I was back living with my dad, the monster. He was okay for a while; he was lying low and keeping his head down. The authorities had now been alerted and he knew he couldn't send me to school with a single hair out of place. I thought he might take a step back for a while but the beatings and the rapes never really stopped. During one especially traumatic weekend when he raped me repeatedly, I dared to threaten him with Social Services. Dad remained calm and slowly climbed the stairs. He returned with a bottle of pills that he emptied out on the table and started to line them up in a neat row.

'You've fucking ruined my life you have; everything is your fault.'

'Dad what are you doing?'

'What does it look like?'

He was counting the tablets, 'four, five, six, seven.'

He counted them; twenty-four in all.

'The books say that twenty is enough to kill you so I'm just making sure.'

'Dad, what are you doing?'

He looked up with a frown. 'I'm killing myself you stupid little cow, what do you think I'm doing?'

'No Dad,' I lunged for the pills but he smacked my hand away.'

Suddenly the thought of my dad dying and leaving me all alone was more than I could bear.

'You've ruined my life,' he repeated.

'I haven't Daddy, I'm sorry.'

He tipped another pile of tablets on the table and started lining them up. My mouth fell open. The suggestion was obvious.

'Perhaps it's better if we both died.'

I couldn't speak.
'Or would you rather go and live with your mother?'
My defence and survival mechanism kicked in. I didn't want to die. 'I want to live with you, Dad.'
'Are you sure?'
'Yes Daddy, I'm sure.'
Over the next hour Dad played out his little suicide game. He even managed to swallow half a dozen pills just to jack up the drama a little but I don't think it was ever his intention to kill either of us that day. It was just another form of psychological torture. But I have no doubt he was capable of killing, because he talked about it often enough and he had already killed once before. Once again I returned to school and once again the faces turned away from me. I waited for the knock on the door that never came.

16

Pregnant For The Second Time

I was twelve years old. The summer was drawing to an end and the nights were getting cold. Dad was regularly raping me sometimes four times a day. We had a gym set up in the lounge and there was a big gym ball that we used to do stretches over. One evening, Dad told me to strip. He wanted sex and this time he rolled the gym ball over to me. I told him I didn't feel well but that didn't stop him - it never did. He started to have sex with me and almost immediately I started to feel sick.

'Dad, Dad, stop, I'm going to be sick.'

'Shut the fuck up.'

I projectile vomited all over the lounge and sofa, retching and choking as I struggled to catch my breath. The smell was awful and I clawed at the ball as I tried to push myself up. A memory that will stay with me forever is that the sick psychopath didn't break stride. He simply pushed my face back onto the spew covered gym ball and continued to take his pleasure for another five minutes. As he finished I slipped from the ball and landed in a pool of my own vomit. He buckled up his trousers and walked away. As he reached the doorway he turned around and said, 'Get that fucking mess cleaned up.'

I saw Mom in town a few days later. I hadn't seen my brother and sister for a long time, but I couldn't muster any enthusiasm when I saw them. Part of me blamed my mom for what was happening to me, because she had made no secret of the fact that she didn't want me. She had given me away when I was six years old and been absent from most of my life ever since. There were days out of course, and we would catch up at family parties but other than that there was very little contact.

We were in the queue at the bank and I turned to my mother, 'Mom, why don't you get back together with Dad and then everything will be fine again, I won't keep getting hurt.'

She stared at me, 'what do you mean?'

'He hurts me Mom,' I said.

'He hurts you?'

'Yes, he hurts me really badly and I just want to live a normal life like other girls.'

'What do you mean he hurts you? In what way?'

I think Mom knew. She finished in the bank and took me into a little coffee shop where we sat down and talked. I cried most of the time, begging her to come back and believing everything would be okay if she did. Mom said that she had a really nice social worker, a young man in his twenties. She told me she would speak to him and get him to file an official complaint against Dad.

'You're sure that's what you want?' she asked.

'Yes Mom.'

I saw her again in town a few days later and she said that the complaint had been filed. I waited for a knock on the door. Surely they wouldn't let me down this time. A week later I met Mom while my Dad was at work and she handed me a one-page letter.

'Don't bother reading it, just read the last line,' she said.

I took the letter from her. I skipped over the letter and read words like investigate and visits and social workers' reports and then I read the last two lines:

We have no concerns over the wellbeing and safety of Shannon. We believe she is living in a safe environment and we will not be taking any further action.

I was being sick most mornings and my stomach was starting to swell again. It was hard and I knew the familiar signs all too well. I was pregnant again, possibly three months along. This time I was determined to keep my child; this time the monster wouldn't get anywhere near it. I would hide, I would run, I would do anything possible to keep him away for me and I began to make plans about how I would escape and where I would go.

Nature intervened during this second pregnancy when I was twelve years old and while Dad was at work on nightshift I endured three hours of indescribable agony and cramps curled up in a ball on the sofa. Just when I thought I couldn't bear the pain any longer I started to bleed and rushed to the toilet. I sat there for over an hour while what looked like clotted blood fell into the toilet. I knew what was happening, because I had read about it on Google. My baby was dead and I was miscarrying.

Dad and I were in town and he sent me to the café where Mom would often go to. She was a regular customer and went there most days. Dad said he hadn't seen my sister for a long time and although he didn't want to see Mom he did want to see my sister.

'Just come back and tell me if Chloe is there.' he said. 'Be back here in five minutes.'

I left him and walked around the corner to the café. Sure enough, Mom was there but all on her own. As she spotted me her face lit up and she held out her arms. I fell into them and broke down in tears.

'What's wrong?' she asked.

It took me some time before I could speak but I told her about some of the beatings my dad was giving me. I begged her to come and help me, to take me away from the horrors I was suffering on a daily basis. The more I told her the more I kept crying and I completely forgot about the five minutes my father had allowed me. Dad appeared in the doorway, his face like thunder. The café was fairly busy and he started shouting at the top of his voice, swearing and cursing and accusing me of crying to my mommy. He grabbed my arm and started dragging me away. Mom tried to intervene, but he told her that if she took another step towards him he would do her some serious damage. As if to make a point he took a step towards her and spat in her face. It was disgusting and as the saliva dripped from Mom's chin he pulled me out of the shop doorway. He dragged me around the corner out of sight of the crowded café and slapped me hard across the face.

'Don't you ever fucking do that again!' he screamed.

'Do what?' I protested.

'Cry on that bitch's shoulder.'

'But…'

'What the fuck were you talking about?'

'Nothing.'

'Then why were you fucking crying?'

He slapped me again and dragged me back home.

We passed people in the street and I was crying as he pulled me along. Some looked, most turned their heads away and nobody helped me. Someone in the café had telephoned the police and persuaded Mom to file a complaint so within ten minutes of reaching home the police were there in force. There were dozens of them and three riot vans were parked in the street. I dared to hope that perhaps he would be locked up and that I would be able to live with Mom again. Dad went quietly and the police left me on my own. The news got better and I heard that my mom and my auntie had also accused him of having raped them in the past. The police told him that he would be charged with battery and the application of unlawful force or common assault, any of which carried a prison sentence. There were witnesses and this time he couldn't hide. I was all on my own that night but I slept well. I was convinced my Mom would come for me the next morning and take me back to live with her, but instead, my dad walked through the door just after midday. The police had charged him with common assault but incredibly they let him go.

There were some inconsistencies in Mum and Aunt's

story and he wasn't going to be charged with rape. Once again, there was no evidence and it was his word against theirs.

Dad didn't get jail, instead he got small fine and Mom received £20 compensation. What a waste of time. To this day I'm astounded that he wasn't sent to jail that time. He had already been jailed for GBH against my mother and there was an old restraining order against him and now he had gone and assaulted her again, this time in public. What the hell was the judge thinking? If he had been jailed my life may have taken another direction. The monster had returned with a slap on the wrist and he was free to do as he wanted yet again. That same evening he ordered me into his bed and raped me.

A month later I knew for sure I was pregnant again. At thirteen I was already well experienced when it came to pregnancy and my stomach was starting to show. Dad suspected I was pregnant, because one night in bed he noticed that my stomach was sticking out despite my fairly strict exercise regime.

'You'll have to get an abortion.'

I said nothing, I hated the idea of abortion. I still do, but if I disagreed with Dad I knew it would end up in a beating.

'We can't go to the doctors or the hospital but I'll find someone to do it.'

I wondered how much more pain I could take. After everything he'd put me through he now wanted me to get rid of my child with a back-street abortion.

A few weeks later I went to school feeling particularly low and I was sick in the toilets before class even started. A friend walked in when I was washing my face.

'My God Shannon, you look like shit. What's wrong?'
I stood up and faced her. She was a good friend and at that moment I wondered if I could trust her.
'Can you keep as secret?' I asked.
'Of course I can, what is it.'
'I'm pregnant.'
Her mouth fell open and she stared at my stomach.
'Fucking hell. You sure?'
I nodded. I didn't want to tell her how familiar I was with pregnancy but instead I lifted my shirt and showed her my bump.
'You won't tell anyone, will you?'
'You can trust me.'
Within a few days every girl in the school knew Shannon Clifton was pregnant and it was only a matter of time before the news filtered down to the teachers.
The school nurse came for me and we went into her office. She asked me questions about my periods and then lifted my shirt and examined my stomach. Although she suspected I was pregnant she said we needed to do a pregnancy test to make sure, I refused. Somehow that would have made it official and that frightened me.
'I'm not pregnant,' I said.
'You told your friend.'
'I didn't, she's making it up.'
I kept denying it. The nurse kept pushing me to do a test.
'If you're pregnant we will need to tell your father.'
'I'm not pregnant.'
'I think you are.'
'Have you slept with any boys?'

'No, no way.'
I was panicking and I wished I hadn't told my friend. This was going to end badly.
'We'll ask your Dad if we can do a pregnancy test.'
'No way,' I said, 'he'll bloody kill me if he thinks I'm pregnant.'
'No he won't Shannon, stop being dramatic.'
I begged her not to tell him. They knew exactly what he was like, they had witnessed his violence first-hand and so I made her promise and she agreed.
'Okay, we won't tell him yet, but eventually he will find out.'
She asked me again if I would take a pregnancy test but I shook my head.
'I'm not pregnant, it's impossible.'
I left the office in tears but made the nurse promise again not to mention anything to my father and yet I felt that she knew and that she would be duty bound to report it. Was it out in the open, would someone take some action at last? The nurse and the school never mentioned it again. Dad knew he couldn't beat the baby out of me this time because it was plainly obvious that I was pregnant and he suspected that others were aware of it too. He had another plan; he would exercise the baby out of me. By now, Dad had stopped going to work and he set me a ridiculous training regime that was a combination of gymnastics exercise and kick boxing training. He made me get out of bed at four o'clock and after an hour of stretching, he would make me run and skip for over an hour. Then it was weights and circuit training right up until breakfast. He made me do thousands of press ups and sit ups and repetitions of pull-ups on a bar we had in the doorway. He made

me train until it was time to go to school or until I collapsed onto the floor. Bizarrely, I believe it was this training regime that made me fit and strong enough to hold on to my baby and Dad's plan backfired on him. He was trying to make me miscarry and his torturous training regime just about broke me. When I thought I couldn't take any more he would drag me up from the floor and make me lift more weights or do more pull-ups and squats. One day he made me do 500 squats until my legs eventually buckled and even when he lifted me up my body refused to cooperate and I simply collapsed to the floor again.

We sparred too. With gloves. This time dad wasn't going to take any chances and he left no marks or bruises but we would sometimes go full-on for ten three-minute rounds. It was my chance to take out my frustrations on him and I always gave as good as I got, but Dad always won. He was bigger and stronger and his reach was at least six inches longer than mine so he would keep me at a distance and move in for the kill two or three times in each round and batter the hell out of me. He would hit me at full force in the stomach, but I learned to protect myself by covering up with my elbows. He wasn't going to beat me this time, I would protect my baby with everything I had. Only someone who has boxed before can appreciate the physical and mental strength needed to stand toe to toe in a fight or in a boxing ring and survive a three-minute onslaught. Times that by ten and understand that it's a child versus an adult and that might give you an idea of what condition I was in at the end of those ten rounds. This training regime continued day after day and we were up at four o'clock nearly every morning. During the school holidays Dad kept me in the house and I was going stir crazy sitting at the window looking out at people going about their business or kids playing in the street. I should be one of those kids I thought, I should be out playing on a bike or running through the park. Dad had bought me a couple of baggy jumpers that I had to wear whenever he took me out shopping. That was the only time he ever took me out and only if I pleaded with him. We'd walk around the supermarket and he'd make me stand close to him, paranoid that someone would notice me or talk to me.

His training regime continued day after day, but my stomach continued to get bigger and bigger. I was six months pregnant and my father was still raping me every day.

My Nan and my auntie had phoned me and said they were coming around as they had presents for me, but Dad wasn't having any of that. By now I was really starting to show and it was a very hot day so the fact that I was wearing a baggy jumper would give the game away. Nan and Auntie said they were coming around at midday so at eleven o'clock Dad took me out. We didn't have the car at that point so he made me walk. We walked for about an hour and ended up in Derby city centre at the shops.

Nan called Dad at one o'clock and he made up a story about deciding to take me out for the day as a treat. He ended the call by saying they could come and see me during the week but I knew he would never let that happen. My father was still raping me despite the fact I was heavily pregnant. I begged him to stop, convinced it would be doing damage to the baby but he wouldn't listen. After one particularly savage rape I felt I couldn't continue and ran downstairs in hysterics. I was at the end of my tether, I felt suicidal and when I got into the kitchen I opened the drawer and reached for the biggest knife I could find. As Dad came in after me I turned the knife around and pushed the blade tip into my left breast. If I pushed hard enough the blade would pierce my heart and it would all be over. It was a pleasant thought.

Dad was pleading with me. 'Don't do it, I won't ever hurt you again.'

I had heard the same statement a thousand times.

'Everything will be fine; I will sort it.'

Empty words.

'I promise.'

That word again...the nothing word.

I was a split second away from plunging the knife into me when other thoughts began entering my head. I thought about my unborn baby. What if the baby survived, what if Dad cut it out of me and it lived? What if Dad kept it, what if he gave my baby the same sort of existence as I had? The thought of my baby being tortured as much as I had was more than I could bear. I sank to my knees crying and the knife dropped to the floor. I knew I couldn't do that to my unborn child. I didn't fear death or dying or suicide but I made a pledge that my child would be safe and taken care of before I ever went down that road again. I would make sure that it was as far away as possible from the monster in our midst.

Before I had even given birth to my child I had developed a bond with him. I say him because I always felt it would be a boy. Knowing who his father was hard but he was my baby and I had to be his mom. I will always remember the first time I felt a little kick and knew it was my job to keep him safe. I vowed that I would never allow the monster to take another life from me. Whatever it took I was going to keep him safe and I felt a strength within me that I didn't know I had. I was getting stronger by the day and my strength was coming from the baby growing inside me. I had to be strong, I couldn't give up hope.

After the holidays, I went back to school. There was no hiding my bump now and even a baggy jumper wasn't making any difference. The school knew and therefore the authorities knew so what the hell had they been doing during the holidays? No one had come near the house apart from one social worker who never mentioned the pregnancy. Dad was a nervous wreck as he dropped me off and for the first time ever I saw him look afraid. He told me to walk around with folders in front of my belly, but he was living in cloud cuckoo land if he thought he could hide it any longer. The following week they called me into the office and the nurse I knew from the alternative school I was in before was there. I liked her, she had been nice to me and the authorities had brought her in thinking she might get more out of me. I often wondered if they suspected who the father was before now, but if they did they never disclosed it. She asked me to take a pregnancy test and I refused again. I said I wasn't pregnant.

'Can you tell me anything about the father?' she asked.

I lowered my head and stared at the floor.

'Do you know who the father is?'

I said nothing.

'Someone told us it could be your father's child.'

I said nothing.

'They said you have never dated any boys, not ever. They said you never go out and you are always locked up at home.'

I felt a bead of sweat run down my spine.

The nurse reached forward and tried to lift my jumper up but I knocked her hand away. Someone else came into the office and they fired more questions at me, all the while asking me to do a pregnancy test and in the end I couldn't stand it any longer. I told them I had to go to the toilet and walked down the corridor, past the toilets, went out of the school gates and walked home. I found Dad in our bedroom and I told him what had happened, what the nurse had said and about the questions they were asking me about the father. He sat on the edge of the bed and for once he wasn't shouting and screaming at me. He was quiet and he looked scared. He buried his face in his hands for a while and then looked up. He sighed deeply.

'I'm going to get sent down for a long time,' he said.

I didn't know what he meant.

The next day at school I was called into the office again. This time a policewoman and Social Services were there, asking the same questions as the nurse had the day before. I clammed up and refused to speak. They went on and on, and again they wanted me to do a pregnancy test.

The policewoman moved forward.

'You're not leaving this office until we know for sure.'

That was it, I snapped and I started to scream.

I screamed for about ages. Constantly. I never let up. I told them I wanted to go home. Eventually the social worker, a man, said to the policewoman that it was better to let me go as they weren't getting anywhere. Someone opened the door and I ran out into the corridor and all the way home.

Within an hour the police were knocking on the door of our house, but Dad wouldn't let them in. I thought they might break the door down like I had seen on the TV programmes but after a while they went away. A couple of days later they were back and this time there were four cars and a van parked further up the street. We were watching from the bedroom window. A policeman came into the garden and walked up to the door. He knocked on the door and Dad packed a few things in a rucksack and handed me another rucksack.

'Here are some things you'll need.'

The policeman was shouting through the letter box.

'Mr Clifton we know you are in there and if you don't let us in, my men will force the door!'

We walked down the stairs and stood in the hallway.

'Just a minute!' my dad called out to the policeman.

He stood motionless for a few seconds and then took me by the hand and pulled me towards the back door and I realised that we weren't going to open the door for the police; we were heading in the opposite direction. We were going on the run.

'Dad no, it's over,' I said, 'open the door, let's go back.'

He grabbed at me roughly.

'Get over the fucking fence.'

I looked up. The fence was six feet tall and I was eight and a half months pregnant, but before I could gather my thoughts, he was pushing me over the fence. I'd been through the worst shit anyone could possibly imagine and just when I thought it couldn't get any more dramatic, I was now being kidnapped.

17

Kidnapped

We went on the run. Dad had no real plan and our first stop was at a nearby cashpoint where he drew out the maximum amount allowed. I think it was £300. He said it would be the only withdrawal as the police would be able to track our movements. We walked throughout the night, keeping off the main roads and walking mostly through parks and across fields and once through a dense forest. Dad appeared to know where he was going but although I asked him many times, he never replied. I was completely exhausted and at one point I couldn't walk another step so we lay down on some park benches and I think I slept for a couple of hours. It was the cold that woke me up. I had never been so cold in all my life so when the shops opened, Dad bought me a blanket. We were in a small town somewhere and we got on a bus to Matlock. I slept on the bus as it was nice and warm and the sun shone through the windows, making it even hotter. We got to Matlock and started walking again. We walked for miles and I became aware of a dull but constant ache in my lower torso. I guessed it was the start of the labour pains I had read about when searching on Google.

'Dad, we need to get to a hospital.'

'Keep walking.'

'Where are we going?'

He ignored me.

I assumed that our destination was a friend or relative of Dad's who maybe lived in this area. We would stay with that person and perhaps I could go and have the baby at a hospital where the police were not looking for us. I now know Dad never had no plan and he didn't have a friend or relative in the area. We were on our own.

We wandered aimlessly for the next few days and the pain was gradually getting worse. I begged him to take me to the hospital, but again he refused. I begged him to find me somewhere to sleep, like a small hotel or a bed and breakfast. He said it was impossible because he didn't have enough cash and he couldn't pay with a card because the police would find us. We walked the whole day, ate at McDonalds and then as soon as we finished we were on our feet again and on the move. The pain was becoming intolerable.

'Please Dad, take me to hospital.'

'There isn't going to be any hospital. I'll deliver the baby and as soon as it's born, I'll kill it.'

This was normal talk from my father. He had talked about killing the baby as soon as he knew I was pregnant. His plans for my baby were horrific and he would describe in detail how easy it would be to strangle or smother it.

It wasn't always like that. Sometimes he said he was going to keep the baby and that we'd run away together. From the way he was talking now I was convinced he was going to kill my baby..

'A new-born baby is very weak,' he said, 'it will take less than a minute to kill it.'

He then described how he would chop my baby into pieces small enough to fit into a blender.

'The blenders these days are great. They're strong enough to break down bones and it all comes out like mush.'

He said he would flush the remains down the toilet.

'Or I could just bury it in the garden,' he said casually, 'we have those paving slabs in our garden and I could lift them and bury the baby under there and then I could extend the brick shed over it.'

'Dad, stop talking like that.'

'Nobody will ever know.'

I lost my temper. 'Of course they'll bloody know dad, everyone knows I'm pregnant, everyone knows I'm about to give birth!'

He paused for a minute and looked deep in thought.

'Perhaps not, then,' he said.

At last I thought I had got through to him and breathed a sigh of relief.

'We can bury it at The Mountings in Matlock, no one will think to look there.'

I'd had enough and broke down again. He took my hand and rubbed it gently, looked at me and smiled.

'I want to marry you.'

'What?'

?I want to marry you. We'll move to a country where

it's legal, where it's nice and hot and we can get married and we will have a family together.'

He had talked about marrying me since I was about nine. He had even researched it on the internet and apparently some countries allowed you to marry your daughter. I remember him talking about India. When I was twelve, he gave me a ring on Valentine's Day and slipped it on my ring finger. He didn't actually say we were engaged but the meaning was obvious.

He pointed to my stomach. 'Not this one though, this one I'm going to flush down the toilet.'

I realised that my father was seriously disturbed. He didn't have any real purpose in life and what he was wishing and hoping for was in the realms of sheer fantasy. It could never happen; he didn't have the means or the intelligence to find us a bed for the night, let alone create a new life abroad. During this time I had many sleepless nights and reflected on my worthless life; a life in which my father had degraded me beyond belief. I recently started studying towards a degree in forensic psychology to try and understand what makes a person a monster. I don't use that word lightly; my father is a monster.

18

Psychopaths Walk Among Us

Before I was born, UK and the rest of the world were rocked by the revelations of what had taken place behind the closed doors of a family home at 25 Cromwell Street in Gloucester in the UK. The house what would become known as the House of Horrors, was the home of Fred and Rose West and their children.

I have read extensively about what these parents put their children through for years and I see some unnerving similarities between Fred West's treatment of his daughters and my father's treatment of me. Fred was a monster who started to abuse girls when he was a young adolescent and incredibly, his crusade of depravity against young girls and women spans more than forty years. In chapter one I spoke about my own dysfunctional family where rape, incest and brutality were considered normal behaviour to some of them. Fred West's upbringing was no less brutal and no less depraved but when he was interviewed about his criminal career he shrugged it off as if it were part of normal life.

Fred said he was introduced to sex by his mother at around twelve years of age and admitted to having engaged in acts of bestiality in his early teens. He said that incest was a part of normal family life and claimed that his father slept with several of his sisters. As early as 1957, when Fred was only 16, he was molesting women 'aggressively' (as the locals put it) at a youth club in Ledbury, close to his home in Much Marcle in Herefordshire. His idea of courtship was simply to approach teenage girls and to start groping them. In one well documented incident, he groped a girl on a fire escape outside the youth club and the girl punched him in the face and sent him flying. He fell two stories and landed on his head. Some reporters have stated that he was never the same after that, even suggested that it was that head injury that somehow 'turned' him and was responsible for the creation of the monster that was Fred West. I believe Fred's life was mapped out for him long before the punch that sent him tumbling over those railings.

I have already documented the incest which took place within my father's family. A chill ran down my spine, when I read that Fred's 13-year-old sister told her mother in 1961 that Fred had been raping her for several months. She told her mother she was pregnant and that Fred was the father. He was arrested and incredibly, he openly admitted to police that he had been molesting young girls since his early teens and what was the big deal about sleeping with your sister? The police were astonished when Fred brazenly stated, 'everybody does it,' as if it's a part of normal human behaviour. The case was set for trial and although Fred's mother, Daisy, was said to have been disgusted with what her son had been doing to her daughter, she was prepared to testify in his defence. The case collapsed when his sister unexpectedly refused to testify against him, but in the eyes of the family, Fred was guilty as charged and his mother banished him from the family home so he moved into the Much Marcle house of his aunt Violet. Fred met Rose West when she was just fifteen and because he was twenty-eight, her parents refused to accept the relationship. They soon realised that Fred and Rose were having sex and reported him to Gloucestershire Social Services. It was also rumoured that Rose was engaging in prostitution at Fred's caravan. Unknown to anyone at the time, Fred had met his equal when it came to depravity and the two monsters were to create an almost unbreakable bond. Rose's family too, were about as dysfunctional as it comes. Her father, Bill Letts, was a paranoid schizophrenic and a cruel and sadistic bully who thought nothing of torturing members of his family. It was common knowledge that he sexually groomed Rose from a young age and because of this she escaped the beatings he dished out to her brothers. By the age of 13, Rose was sexually abusing her two younger brothers, again believing the behaviour was 'normal.' When Rose gave birth to their first child, Heather Ann, it was speculated that Bill was the father . This was extremely painful for me to read, because it makes me wonder just how many of these fathers are out there. It's this so called 'normalised' sexual behaviour of young exploited and vulnerable girls that tears my heart to pieces. Fred and Rose West's daughters went through unimaginable horrors and according to one of the daughters, Anna Marie West, her and her sister Charmaine were subjected to beatings and torture from a young age. A childhood friend of Charmaine's remembered an incident when she had entered the Wests' home and found Charmaine naked and with her hands tied behind her back while Rose stood next to her with a large wooden spoon in her hand. It was clear by the marks on her body that the child had been beaten with the spoon. The girl said that the gravity of the situation she was witnessing took her breath away, but the reaction of the two West daughters shocked her more than anything. The naked Charmaine looked calm and unconcerned and Anna Marie had a blank expression on her face, as if it were just another day in the West family home. The West children had to do most of the household upkeep from a young age, something my father made me do too.

They were seldom allowed to socialise outside the home unless either Fred or Rose were present. Again, although not exactly locked up because I did attend several out of school activities, my Father never left me there alone and he controlled them to the extent that if he couldn't be there in person then he wouldn't let me go. The only time I was ever allowed out of the house alone was during that three-day camping trip to the Peak District. Dad took me to school and collected me almost every day and the West children also had to follow strict guidelines imposed by their parents, with severe physical punishment meted out if they broke any of the household rules. The violence dished out by Fred West was often irrational or just inflicted for the hell of it and it mirrors exactly the actions of my father. Between 1972 and 1992, the West children were admitted to the accident and emergency departments of local hospitals an incredible 31 times and not once were these injuries ever reported to Social Services. Again, we have to ask the question why? I was also admitted to hospital with suspicious injuries and nothing ever came of it. I cried buckets when I read about poor eight-year-old Anna Marie West. The two depraved freaks took her to the cellar at 25 Cromwell Street, where the child was stripped naked, bound to a mattress and gagged before Fred raped her as his wife looked on and encouraged him. After the rape Fred explained that it was a father's job to do that to their daughter. The hairs stood up on the back of my neck.

Then Fred said, 'Don't say anything to anybody.'

They forced poor Anna Marie to perform household chores while dressed in skimpy outfits and miniskirts. More similarities with my own abuse. They also forced her to drink wine and I remember how my father made me drink alcohol. Even now this doesn't make any sense to me. I told my father all the time that I didn't like the taste of the drinks or the effect they had on me and alcohol isn't cheap so just what was it that Fred West and my father got out of forcing their daughters to get drunk?

Around this time Fred and Rose had befriended a young hitchhiker, Caroline Owens. She started living at Cromwell Street and after a particularly vicious sexual assault she escaped, but Fred and Rose tracked her down and recaptured her. Fred threatened that he would keep her locked in the cellar forever and when they were finished with her, he'd bury her under the patio 'with the others.' Owens knew she had to escape before the Wests killed her so she agreed to stay on as their housekeeper and sexual plaything. Her plan worked out and she managed to escape when she was at a launderette. She made it back to her mother's house and at first she was too ashamed to disclose the horrors that had taken place in the West's house but her mother was concerned at the amount of injuries on her body. Eventually she broke down and told her mother what had happened and she immediately contacted the police. The Wests were arrested and charged with rape, assault, indecent assault and actual bodily harm and they were told that they could both go to prison for life.

Their reign of terror could so easily have come to an end at that point.

The case was due to be tried at Gloucester Magistrates Court on 12 January 1973. It's worth bearing in mind that this wasn't Fred West's first conviction. He already had a string of offences to his name, including child molestation, indecent assault, theft and sexual assault.

At the last-minute Caroline Owens decided she couldn't face the ordeal of testifying in open court and all charges relating to sexual abuse were dropped. The Wests pleaded guilty to the lesser charged of indecent assault and actual bodily harm.

What happened next will surely go down as the most flawed decision by a magistrate in British Legal history: Fred and Rose West were fined £50 and allowed to walk free.

It defies logic! This is a crime for which the perpetrators should have been jailed for at least seven years. Remember, the Wests admitted guilt and Fred had a previous conviction relating to sexual assault. They must have walked out of court thanking their lucky stars and wondering what the hell had just happened. When Caroline Owens heard the news it broke her and she attempted suicide. The law and the authorities had let her down.

I knew exactly how she felt.

Three months later the Wests committed their first known murder, that of 19-year-old Lynda Gough. They would go on to kill at least another eleven people though experts agree that the real number of victims is probably much higher.

Reading about the Wests and the magistrate's decision tears me to pieces. As with my father, the authorities failed to act despite all the evidence thrown in their faces. My father was a monster and so were the Wests but it was the authorities who let me down and it was the authorities who were to blame for the countless deaths of poor, vulnerable girls in the West Country spanning twenty years. They knew. They all knew. Why did they fail to act?

In recent weeks I have learned about another father who abused and raped his daughter, an Austrian called Josef Fritzl.

Fritzl imprisoned his daughter for twenty-four years in a basement cellar under his own house. It was thirty-five meters square, barely high enough for her to stand up, and Josef Fritzl raped her at will for the entire period of her captivity. He was another bully, who ruled his house with a rod of iron. The signs were there for all to see. The Austrian authorities failed to notice the sexual and physical abuse poor Elizabeth suffered as a child. Or did they? Was this a similar case to that of my own? Did they know? Did they turn a blind eye like they had in the case of Fred and Rose West? Was the easiest course of action to look the other way? Even in my own immediate family, I guessed that some of them suspected what was going on behind closed doors, but was it too horrific to even contemplate? Was it just so unimaginable that a father was raping his own daughter that they ignored their own suspicions? I believe there's a bit of truth in that.

At times I sat down with my Mom but couldn't quite get the words out, couldn't tell her exactly what was going on. She knew that he was beating me, she'd seen the black eyes, the bruises, the broken nose and that was bad enough but there was a line that I believe she didn't want to cross; she couldn't bring herself to believe that her little girl was being raped by her father.

Could Fritzl's wife Rosemarie have thought the same way? She has been cleared of any wrongdoing, because the authorities believe that she knew nothing of her daughter's twenty-four years of captivity barely a few meters under the floorboards she walked every day.

It's hard to believe.

Fritzl disappeared for hours while he was in that cellar and at one point he was supplying groceries for up to eight people. He needed gas to cook and cleaning materials, plates and pans. Fritzl was clever. Whenever he shopped for items like baby clothes, nappies and infant food he made sure that he shopped in the other side of town, in a district where nobody knew him. Astute yes, but nobody is going to convince me that not once, in twenty-four years, did Rosemarie see him carrying groceries into that cellar. Even if he only shopped once a week that would be 1,250 times that he carried groceries into the cellar.

Fritzl was a bully, that was well documented, was it that his own wife was so terrified of him that she actually knew about her own daughter being kept as a prisoner below their house? I suspect it was. Was it the same fear that stopped so many of the authorities in Derbyshire stepping in to rescue me?

The only reason my abuse came to light was because it could not be hidden any longer.

There were dozens of similarities between my abuse and Elizabeth's. Fritzl kept his daughter indoors during her childhood, he never let friends into the house and boyfriends were strictly off limits. During one interview with a former friend of Elizabeth's, she said that when the rest of the girls were discussing the 'cute, good looking' boys in the school, Elizabeth didn't want to know and never joined in the conversation. From my own experience I sense that was because her father probably beat that out of her. My father was so jealous when anyone mentioned boys and battered the hell out of me on at least a dozen occasions because he thought I had got too close or too friendly with boys at school. I was a prisoner just like Elizabeth. Although there was no basement, I was still a prisoner in my own home.

Time and time again the system lets the victim down. Just two years prior to Elizabeth's escape in 2006, another Austrian girl, Natascha Kampusch also escaped an underground prison where she had been held captive by Wolfgang Priklopil. She had been kidnapped in 1998 by a man in a 'white minibus van' in Vienna. The Vienna police, over the next week interviewed 776 drivers and registered owners of similar types of van and Priklopil was amongst them. They asked him if he could provide an alibi for the day of the kidnapping. He shook his head and told officers he was home alone that day, he saw no one. They inspected his van but were apparently satisfied with his explanation that he only used his rather grotty vehicle to move building rubble and they left.

A few days later, a tip came in from a police dog handler who gave a description of a man and the address of the large house he lived in. He was known as a loner with an unhealthy sexual interest in young girls. The alarm bells should have been ringing loudly at that point. He had surveillance cameras outside his property and it was mentioned that he may even be hiding weapons there. The property was registered in the name of Priklopil's mother and he lived there - the man with the white minibus van. The computer showed that he had been interviewed already and the police decided there was little point interviewing him a second time. The report was filed and forgotten. That forgotten report cost Natascha Kampusch, eight years of her life.

19

My Baby Boy, My Father's Child

I had one decent night's sleep during the five days we were on the run and that was when we slept in the waiting room of Matlock Station. We arrived at midnight and the centrally heated room was warm and inviting. There was nobody around, just me and dad. We took it in turns to sleep, because Dad was worried the police might turn up. In the small hours of the morning he said I could sleep for the rest of the night and I went out like a light and slept until six when the first commuters of the day began to drift in. We walked along a platform and through the concourse and I saw a newspaper stand. The front page of the local newspaper carried my photograph with the headline: 'MISSING.'

Dad bought the paper and quickly walked away. The police had put out an urgent appeal, because I had been missing for some days and they were concerned for my safety.

'We need to get out of here,' he said and threw the paper into a bin.

The pain had started again and I pleaded with him to take me to hospital but he ignored me again. Dad's behaviour was becoming more irrational. He worked out that because he'd seen the newspaper in Matlock we had to get away from the area as quickly as possible. It was a Derbyshire local paper so I assumed we would be heading south to London or maybe even to Scotland where we could blend in and hide.

Dad decided we would head back to Derby.

I didn't argue, because I wanted to get caught. Dad made up the name James Lillieshaw and said that if the police caught us, I had to tell them James Lillieshaw was the father.

'Yes Dad.'

We took the bus direct into the city centre. I complained that we hadn't washed for four days; I hadn't even pulled a brush through my hair. Dad didn't care but I pointed out that we looked like tramps and people were starting to notice us so he said he had a plan. In Derby we went into DW Sports Leisure Centre. We walked straight in and Dad told me to go into the changing rooms of the leisure centre and have a wash. I washed my face and then awkwardly stuck my head under the tap and managed to shampoo my hair with some of the liquid hand wash. By the time I had changed and rubbed my hair a bit drier I could feel he cramps coming back again.

Dad was waiting for me outside. He clearly hadn't showered and with five days beard growth he

looked a mess. He had been guarding the exit to the changing rooms, scared that I would run away.
'I need to get to hospital, Dad.'
He said we needed to get to a supermarket and do some shopping.
As we stood in a checkout with our groceries there was a woman looking at something on her mobile phone and she would keep looking up at us and then look back at the phone. It was clear that she was looking online at the same article we had seen in Matlock train station. While we were being served at the checkout the woman walked away with the phone to her ear. She stood in the doorway she turned around to look at us. She was talking to someone and wouldn't take her eyes off us. Dad freaked out after we got through the checkout and we were almost running by the time we got outside. For some reason Dad figured we would be inconspicuous in Pride Park, a huge industrial outlet complex. When we arrived I noticed several police cars driving around the area looking for us. We ran down one of the small offshoots of the business park and turned the corner past one of the industrial units. It was a dead end and by now Dad was in a right state. I begged him to give us up to the police so that I could go to hospital, but he grabbed my arm and pulled me behind the back of a building. We looked towards the top of the street and saw a police car pull up. Two policemen got out and then two more ran over and started to speak to their colleagues. Dad told me to be quiet.
'Please dad, take me to the hospital.'
'Shut the fuck up and be quiet.'
To my dismay, the policemen climbed into the car

ten minutes later and drove away. Dad was smiling from ear to ear because he thought his plan had worked. We left our makeshift hiding place and walked down the street. A hundred yards later, a plain white car drove towards us, slowed down and stopped. Two men got out and one of them held up a silver badge and identified himself. They were plain clothes policemen.

'Don't move an inch Mr Clifton, you're under arrest.'

Dad turned and pushed me away.

'Run!' he shouted at the top of his voice.

I wasn't going anywhere. I was terrified and I was about to give birth, and he wanted me to outrun two fit policemen. At first I refused to get into the car and when one of them grabbed me I started to kick him. It was a no contest and he quickly had me in the back of the car. I was so frightened I peed myself. Dad didn't run either and to my surprise he gave up rather meekly and climbed into the back of the car. In the meantime another police car had pulled up and they pushed me into the second car to separate us. I have never been so frightened in my life and for a while I cried for my Dad, begging the policemen to let me be with him. During the short drive to the police station I came to realise that it was all over and although I wanted to be with Dad, I was also relieved that the eight years of hell at the hands of my father were about to come to an end.

They took me to a police station that didn't look anything like a police station. It was nicely furnished with watercolour paintings on the walls and there wasn't a police uniform in sight.

I went into a room with a policewoman and asked her for some Paracetamol, because my pain was back with a vengeance. She questioned me about the father of my child and I stuck to my story and refused to tell them I was pregnant. However, as time passed by, it became obvious that they knew everything and I also knew that it might only be a few hours before I gave birth. It was the pain that made me finally give in and admit I was pregnant. I gave them the story about the fictitious James Lillieshaw. I was in the police station for three hours and although I was still in pain it was at least bearable. I was placed with a really nice emergency foster family for the night – they even knew my aunties! I went for a bath and one of the daughters plaited my hair and then we had dinner. I was starving and it was the first proper food I'd had for a week. The following morning a police car arrived at the house and they took me to hospital for a scan. It was incredible seeing my baby on the scanner and the nurse pointed out the little hands and feet and I asked if she could tell whether it was a boy or girl.

She shook her head. 'I can't, it's too big.'

She explained that when a baby got to a certain size, their limbs generally hid any clue to their gender. It didn't matter because I knew it was a boy, I had felt it since I first found out I was pregnant.

I told the nurse that I was now in considerable pain and asked for some pain killers. The nurse examined me and thought I was still a few days away from giving birth so she didn't think I was in labour.

Then two policewomen arrived and they took me to a private room in the hospital and started to question me about the father again. To my amazement they told me they had found the alleged father and he denied everything.

'We have him in custody,' the policewoman said. 'He's the only James Lillieshaw in Derby but he says he has never even met you, let alone had a sexual relationship with you and we believe him.'

I looked down at the floor. They knew.

'Do you want to tell us who the real father is?'

I said nothing.

'We interviewed him for three hours, and he's a nice lad, we believe him. We interviewed some of your best friends too and they told us you have never had a boyfriend, not ever. They say you never go anywhere, never go out, not even to a party or a school disco. You never go anywhere; you are always at home with your father.'

There was a long pause during which neither policewomen spoke.

'Some of your friends are saying your father could be the father of your baby,' one of them said eventually.

I didn't answer any more questions after that.

I was taken to hospital and began to have contractions that evening. The pains were horrific and lasted right through the night and into the early hours. One of the nurses ran me a bath and said it would make me more comfortable and it would ease the pain. I climbed into the warm water, sank down and waited for the pain to subside. It didn't work and, if anything, the pain got worse. She helped me out and said I wasn't ready to give birth so I might as well get some sleep. I didn't sleep a wink, because the dull constant ache in my lower back was unbearable and every few minutes I suffered the most agonising spasms and I wondered how long this was going to go on. Later that evening my Mom and my sister Chloe arrived. I was overjoyed because

I hadn't seen my sister for a long time.
They brought me some gifts and toys for the baby and a whole load of beautiful baby clothes. They were plain white hats and baby grows.
My son was born the following day. The delivery was very traumatic and nearly died twice. He kept getting stuck and I kept passing out. The delivery team couldn't get the placenta out because it had attached itself to the walls of my uterus instead of the lining and it made the delivery a whole lot more complicated. I lost a lot of blood and they gave me a transfusion. Retained Placenta is a condition that normally results in an infection that can cause death.
I was drugged up and floating in and out of unconsciousness but at least the pain had eased. I remember a nurse shouting 'it's a boy!' and then I lost consciousness.
When I came around, they let me see my baby. It was a surreal moment and I swear my heart stopped as they placed him on my chest. It seemed like I was in some sort of crazy dream, it didn't seem real. I thought I was going to wake up at any moment and I knew at that point, despite who his father was and how he was conceived, I loved him with all of my heart. They allowed me no more than ten minutes with him and then they whipped me away to theatre.
When I got back from theatre and woke up again I couldn't have been happier as they brought my baby to me and I dressed him. I put a little hat on him that said hello world. The last thing I wanted was for my boy was to have nothing. I held up the tiny clothes and cried tears of joy as my sister hugged me.
The following day the police came to the hospital again and told me my Dad had been released on bail

the previous day. I broke down and cried. How on earth was this possible?

They told me not to worry, the conditions of the bail were that he had to stay away from me and my baby and couldn't come within three miles of the hospital. They took DNA swabs from me and my baby. I was scared. Why the hell had they let Dad out on bail after he kidnapped me and took on the run for five days?

'He won't get near my baby will he?' I asked the policewoman.

'Of course not, Love,' she said, 'everyone who comes in here has to pass the front desk and we have given your dad's name and a description. He's not allowed in under any circumstances.'

Dad came to the hospital and simply gave a false name and said he'd come to see a family friend and her newborn baby. He asked what ward I was on and the receptionist told him.

Luckily, my auntie was in the reception area just then and spotted him. She told two policemen and they challenged him just outside the ward. Dad kicked off and started fighting so one of them tasered him and he was arrested for breaking the conditions of his bail.

Thankfully I was blissfully unaware of this latest drama, because I was fast asleep at the time, exhausted after more than a week without a decent night's sleep.

They locked my dad up and told me this time there was no chance of him being released.

20

DNA Test and Police Interviews

I was in a mother and baby foster placing when one of the staff told me the police were here to see me. I guessed what it was about. The policewoman looked both stern and sympathetic and I knew what was coming.

'The DNA results have come back.'

They had done DNA tests on me, my mom and my dad. I remember thinking at this point, 'I hope I'm bloody adopted.'

I waited. She had difficulty getting out the words but eventually she did.

'Your son is your father's baby.'

I let out a deep breath. 'Tell me something I don't know.'

'He's the only person you slept with?'

The statement sounded ridiculous. Slept with. As if I had a choice.

'Yes.'
My answer to her next question would shape the rest of my life and that of my father's.
'Did he only do it the one time?'
I bit down hard on my lip. I shook my head and she let out a sigh as she too, shook her head.
She reached for my hand. 'How many times, Love?'
'Thousands of times.'
'Thousands of times,' she said, 'surely you're exaggerating?'
I shook my head, 'no, he's been raping me since I was six years old.'
The social worker who was with me in the small office nearly fell off her seat. My Mom was in a room next door, because she was not allowed to be with me in the interview room.
The policewoman and the social worker were stunned.
'From six years old?' the policewoman asked. 'are you sure?'
'One hundred percent sure,' I answered.
I told them about the first time he did it, when he raped me on the floor; I told them how I had begged him to stop and how he had raped me over and over again, almost every day for eight years.
'Every day?' she questioned.
'Yes,' I said, 'sometimes more than once a day, sometimes he would rape me in the morning, in the afternoon and wake me up again during the night and do it again.'
The social worker buried her hands in her face. There were tears running down her face. She was taking it very badly and so she should because she knew about all the complaints and all the visits and the

school reports. We were in there for about an hour that first time but there would be many interviews to follow over the coming weeks.

But they didn't know the half of it because I just couldn't find it in me to tell them all the sordid details: how he had tied me up and beaten me and filmed me and a part of me wanted to protect him. I knew my father was a monster but somehow I didn't want the authorities to think that. I knew that Dad was facing prison, I just didn't know for how long. I felt some sort of relief that it was out in the open.

The social worker asked me if I wanted to see my Mom.

I said yes.

She told me that she would need to see her first and left me with the policewoman, who sat in stunned silence holding my hand. It was thirty minutes before I saw Mom. I walked into the room and could see that she had been crying. She had been in denial for years but I sensed she had suspected all along. She explained that she had told Social Services about the 'weird' relationship for years. She told me she told Social Services that my Dad hadn't had a girlfriend for ten years and that it didn't seem right. Even then, when the social worker told her the DNA results had come back and that my father was the father of my baby, she didn't want to believe it. She sat with her head in her hands. My mother has to share the blame and I think she knew that. She had affectively abandoned me when my father went to prison and then left me in his hands once he was released. It is something that she will have to live with for the rest of her life. I don't blame my mother for what happened to me, because it was my father who did it, but Mom suspected what was happening and although she tried to get the authorities involved, she didn't try hard enough. Mom started asking me questions and I don't think the gravity of what Dad had been doing to me had yet registered with her.

She was sobbing, 'I kept filing complaints but they kept coming back saying that you were fine.'

Mom knew exactly what Dad was capable of - he'd battered her dozens of times and once to within an inch of her life and she had once accused him of rape.

'I'm sorry,' she said over and over again.

I never realised how many times Mom had registered complaints with the authorities. She told me a story of when I was only about six years old and it was the first time she realised he had been beating me. Dad was dropping me off at Nan's while Mom was visiting and she noticed I had a black eye. She asked what had happened to me and I glanced over my shoulder at Dad, who was walking back to the car. Mom snapped and, although she was terrified of Dad, she ran to the garage, returned with a big machete and chased after Dad, threatening to kill him. Luckily, he made it to the car before she reached him and managed to drive away. I can't remember the incident at all even though I was apparently crying hysterically, thinking Mom was going to kill my dad. I suppose it's not surprising though, because I know my brain has blocked out a lot of stuff.

The cat was now out of the bag and in spite of the police telling me I would remain anonymous, I started getting messages from both sides of the family almost straight away.

Sadly, some of Dad's family members chose to ignore me and immediately took his side. I also began getting messages from my friends. How did they know? The police had told me that I had the right to remain anonymous, but it was a nonsense. The anonymity was a charade and everything was public knowledge within 24 hours I wanted to crawl into a hole and die. Not only did everybody know I had a baby, they knew who the father was. One of the reasons I have now waived my anonymity and I'm my story is to put the record straight and to tell it exactly how it was. It wasn't a difficult decision, because it seems the whole of Derbyshire knew anyway who Shannon Clifton is and what her father did to her.

There would be at least six full interviews with the police over the next few weeks. Each one was a torture session where I had to relive everything. My Mom was never allowed to sit in on them; just two policewomen and a social worker.

'I've been pregnant before,' I told them.

'What?'

'Twice,' I said, 'when I was eleven and thirteen.'

I watched as her eyes filled with tears, 'your father's?' she asked.

I nodded silently.

'You lost them both?'

I nodded. I didn't want to go into details. Not yet.

I realised from the outset that these were serious charges, because one policewoman said my dad could be locked up for life. I thought about disclosing the other things he had forced me to do but what was the point? If he was going to get locked away for life there was no need to rake up the very worst things. They had the DNA evidence and that proved everything as far as I was concerned. I remember they tried to get me to go into really graphic detail, wanting to know exactly how everything had happened and they wanted me to disclose very explicit details like the positions he had raped me in. I kept crying when they asked me that. What was the point? I told them that my Dad had raped me for nine years, I told them it had been a regular occurrence and that he'd beat me at the same time. I told them about the black eyes and the split head, I told them he had stabbed me with a screwdriver and I nearly lost an eye when he tried to poke it out with a pen and how he'd made me stand naked in the garden in the rain while he stared at me through the window. I told them so much. Yet I didn't tell them half of what I'd been through. I started to dread each interview. They made me repeat so much of what I'd already told them and the interviews were recorded on camera which made it a complete nightmare.

'Are you sure?' they'd ask. 'Are you certain?'

It was beginning to wear me down and even the social worker intervened several times, berating them for the onslaught they threw at me.

The police took my mobile phone and changed some of the settings. They told me I was unable to speak to members of Dad's family as it might jeopardise any trial or proceedings against him. I couldn't quite understand what they were saying about trials and proceedings as the DNA test had already proven his guilt.

I started to get messages from my Nan - Dad's Mom - and couldn't answer her back. It was heart-breaking because I wanted to speak to her so badly.

Please get in touch with me it's extremely important

And

Why can't you get in touch with me I'm going out of my mind with worry
I'm trying to find out what's going off but nobody will tell me. I got a letter from your dad yesterday he's in prison, I've been sick with worry where are you?

I could sense the frustration and desperation in every word.

Why aren't we allowed to see u?

And then a slight change in attitude.

Still no reply, you are being really rude and ignorant or someone is stopping you from contacting me

Then she started talking more about Dad.

We love you Shannon hope u r okay. Your dad said b strong, he loves you

I've been to see your dad today and he told me about the baby, I'd love to see you both I'm always here for you xxx

Hi Shan, just to tell you I want to see you and the baby so much, your dad is really worried about you he loves you so much

These messages were tearing me to pieces. My dad was telling me he still loved me despite everything he had put me through. I understood that Nan supported Dad because he's her son, but I still found it difficult to cope with. I spoke to the police but they were still adamant I shouldn't speak to Nan; it was as if she was in the enemy camp along with my dad.

If you can't see me for some reason just let me know you are ok.
We're all here for you, love you Shan

Love u Shan

Here for you Shan

I love you Shan wherever you are. There will always have a place in my heart for you and your baby
xxxxx *Love ya Shan*

I won't give up on you, we all love you so much

Hiya Shan, hope you and the baby are well, been trying to contact you for over a month now and still no reply. I'd love to be able to hold you in my arms and tell you things will be alright, you know it's breaking my heart. Please answer me Shannon even if it's just to tell me to piss off.

A few days later Mom told me Nan had been to see Dad in prison. Now she had no doubt because Dad had admitted that he's the father of my child although he had not admitted to raping me or abusing me from the age of six years old. She was different towards me and there were no further questions and I left it at that. I had never told my Mom, the police or the authorities the full story of the wickedness my father had heaped on me because I couldn't talk about it. Thinking about what he had done was bad enough. I harboured enormous secrets and guilt began to creep in. Towards the end of the interviews I did tell the police about the time my family member had raped me when I was five. They arrested him and brought him in for questioning. Sadly, a week later the police told me that there was no evidence to use against him and it was only my word against his and so they let him go.

The family was starting to split in two: Mum's side and Dad's side. There was a clear division and it broke my heart that so many of Dad's brothers and sisters and some of his friends and neighbours supported him via messages directly to me and in posts on social media. How could they do that; he had impregnated his own daughter?

And then something strange started to happen. The public decided to get involved and in certain circles and group chats they were calling our family sick and perverted. People were even starting to blame me and random people were saying that I should burn in hell. Someone else wrote that I deserved everything I got, and that I had asked for it. I was completely stunned and yet I realised that these people only knew that I had been made pregnant by my father, they didn't know the full story. As far as they were concerned, the acts had been consensual; they knew nothing of the abuse that had taken place from an early age. As time passed, the backlash grew stronger. My dad's family took the brunt of it and people called them wicked and evil, they had death threats, their houses were covered in graffiti and people threw bricks and bottles at their windows.

One of my uncles had to move away. This was a dark period for me. I could understand the anger directed towards my dad's family but these people had no right to judge me. Dad's parents, Nan and Grandad also received death threats and horrible, nasty messages and posts on Facebook. People blamed them for bringing up a monster, and it didn't go down well that they were sticking by their incarcerated son. It was clear from the messages Nan was sending me that she was visiting my father in prison and this confused and upset me.

I will always love your dad because a mum's love is unconditional, you'll know this now you are a mum. I hate what he has done and can't forgive him.

It was nearly six weeks before I started messaging her back. The Police had their case and he had been charged with six counts of raping a girl under 13. This confused me, as he had raped me from the age of six and I asked the police about it. They told me that raping a girl under thirteen carried the same sentence regardless of her age. So whether the girl was six or twelve when it happened, the sentence will be the same.

There were more charges:

- sexual assault of a girl under 13 - with penetration
- two charges of raping a girl 13-15 years old

I remember reading the charges and being stunned. That was it? After everything he had put me through!

While I was trying to come to terms with what I read another message from my nan.

Your dad's told me a lot and if I ever see you again I will tell you.

That messaged bugged me so I texted her back.

Nan, what has Dad actually told you?
Do you know who my baby's dad is?

She replied.

Yes it's your dad, I'm broken hearted Shannon that this cud have ever happened. I don't understand why you cudnt have told me. You know I've always been there for you no matter what and I always will be.

Nan stepped up her hatred for my Mum.

Please Shannon don't be fooled by Pat and her fake pretence, just remember all the evil she has done to you in your life. She gave you away at 5 years old and I don't care what excuses she's telling you now. It was her choice to get rid of you and she hated you and treated u like shit locking you in your room to mention a few things. She stopped you seeing your sister which broke your heart.

I so wanted to meet with Nan but they wouldn't let me, nor would they let me meet with any of dad's family and although the police didn't mean to, they drove a huge wedge between the two families.
But I still loved my dad.
I sent a message to Nan.

I still love and I miss him so much but hate him for what he has put me through and I don't think I'll ever be allowed to see him again which really upsets me.

She replied.

I'm terribly sad about the whole situation, I'm crying now because your dad has no one and because you didn't deserve this and I don't know what will happen in the future.

'Your dad has no one'. That hurt me the most. I thought about Dad in that horrible prison and it brought back memories from all those years ago when I had visited him. I now started to regret everything. Why had I said anything? It was all my fault that Dad was in that horrible place.

21

Stockholm Syndrome

Despite everything he did to me, I missed my dad. I have been asked countless times by social workers, policemen, journalists, friends and family why I tried to protect my father after everything he put me through. Not a day goes by when I don't ask myself the same question and yet last year I read about Stockholm Syndrome and although everything didn't automatically click into place, I began to understand it a little more as I read what it was all about.

The name is derived from a failed bank robbery in the early seventies when masked robbers raided a bank in Stockholm, Sweden and took four employees hostage for six days. They were held in the bank's vault during the standoff with the police. By the end of the six days, such a strong bond had developed between the hostages and their captors that they refused to cooperate with the police and they wouldn't testify in court. Psychologists believe that a bond is automatically created in any situation where individuals are thrown together for twenty-four hours a day. Even if the person in charge abuses the person under their control and threatens their very existence, but then displays an act of kindness or protection, the oppressed person clings on to that act of kindness, however small. A bond can form in a matter of days so is it any surprise that a bond developed between me and my father? Despite everything he did to me he still fed and clothed me, took me to school and after school activities and put a roof over my head. In the Stockholm bank siege the captors first threatened the hostages' lives but then decided not to kill them and informed the hostages of their decision. Psychologists say that it would have been a huge relief to the hostages and the feelings of fear and hopelessness turned into feelings of gratitude towards the robbers. As the Stockholm bank siege undoubtedly proved, it takes only a few days for this bond to form, proving that the victim's natural survival instinct trumps the ill feeling towards the person who caused the situation or the abuse in the first place.

Survival, that's what it boils down to. Survival instinct was at the heart of the Stockholm bank siege and the hostages picked up on any act of kindness no matter how small. I was no different and even now, I have more happy memories of my father's random acts of kindness than I do of his abusive treatment of me. Amidst those horrible conditions of imprisonment and confinement in the bank at Stockholm, the hostages learned to respect and even develop a fondness for the very people who held them captive. I'm not saying it's correct, but it shows that there is often nothing one can do about it. These bank workers were educated adults, I was a small girl, what chance did I have?

Probably the most famous case of Stockholm Syndrome was the case of the kidnapped newspaper heiress Patty Hearst, that happened just a year after the Stockholm bank robbery. She was kidnapped by the Symbionese Liberation Army (SLA) during which time she was raped and threatened with death, but during her short captivity something incredible happened. Patty Hearst not only grew to love and respect her kidnappers, but after only two months of captivity she joined the SLA and even helped them rob a California bank to fund their activities. Incredibly, Hearst had switched roles completely and became a wanted fugitive.

22

I Love You Dad

The first time I saw my father again after my baby was born was seven months later at his sentencing at Derby Crown Court. A couple of months before that my solicitor had called and announced rather cheerfully that dad would be pleading guilty to some of the charges against him and therefore there would be no trial.

'It's great news,' she said, 'it means you won't have to testify in court and there will be no pressure on you.'

It slowly registered with me that she had mention sentencing and that surely meant that my father would be going to prison for a very long time. She'd also said he had pleaded guilty to only some of the charges and I asked her what that meant.

She explained that he had pleaded guilty to five very serious charges, each of which could send him to prison for many years.

'But what about all the other offences you said he would be charged with?' I asked.

She explained that there was little point in pursuing the other charges because it wouldn't necessarily mean that he would get more time in jail.

This was an incredibly confusing time for me and emotionally I was very traumatised.

When my baby was five months old, I decided to give him up for adoption and he was taken away from me. We had spent 24 hours a day together and I had an incredibly strong bond with him, but I realised that a fourteen-year-old girl who was in foster care could not look after a little baby. It wasn't fair on him and he deserved better. He deserved not to be raised anywhere near my useless family. It was the right decision. Even now, looking back at my fragile state of mind I do not regret my decision. Of course he would have a better life living anonymously with a respectable family. Living with me would mean growing up in the care system at least until he was old enough to go to school. Everybody would know that he was a child born from rape, and worse, a child born out of an incestuous rape. It would come out sooner or later and I didn't want him to know that. I wanted him to live a normal, carefree existence, free from worry, free from gossip, free from finger pointing and people whispering behind his back. Basically, I didn't want him to know the horrendous circumstances in which he was conceived. It was the most difficult decision I have ever had to make and I cried myself to sleep every night for months, his beautiful little face the last thing in my mind before I eventually

drifted off to sleep.
I was still thinking of my baby when my solicitor said I would get a chance to read my victim impact statement.
'What's that?' I asked.
'Well,' she said, 'before the judge decides on your dad's sentence you get a chance to tell the court what your dad has put you through.'
'Why?'
'Isn't it obvious? The judge needs to know how bad he has been to you.'
'Do I have to?'
'No, but it would be better if you could.'
My solicitor was gently encouraging me to find the courage to stand up in court and eventually I agreed. At least if I stood up in court I would see Dad. I wanted to see him, as bizarre as that may seem. She said if I could stand up in court and tell everybody how bad it had been then he would get more years on his sentence, therein lay the problem: I didn't want my dad to go to jail forever. He was still my dad. I wanted to get angry with him but I couldn't because he had been the only stable influence in my life despite what he had done to me. As the months had passed, it was slowly sinking in just what he had put me through and part of me now wanted him to be punished but part of me didn't. Nothing made any sense to me and I was still in a terrible state because they had taken my baby away. He was all that mattered to me, not my solicitor, not the judge, not my father, not jail time, not prison.
It took me nearly a month to write out the four or five sheets that I took to court. Every time I wrote a sheet or two, I ripped it up and started again. I went

through three of Tesco's lined notepads but eventually I had what I thought I was comfortable with and even though I knew it was going to be difficult to stand up in court and read it, I knew it was the right thing to do. I wondered where my father would be when I read it, whether he could see me, whether I could see him and what his reaction would be. He would be angry, that's for sure. He was always angry.

When I walked into court, I noticed Dad behind a glass screen. I looked over to him but he wouldn't look in my direction. He knew where I was, he couldn't have failed to notice the commotion as I walked into court with my solicitor and I was annoyed and frustrated that he wouldn't look towards me. The barristers and the judge were very straight faced and stern and the proceedings commenced. I was aware that Mom and some of my aunties were in the public gallery and also some faces and journalists whom I recognised. I was in a daze and I didn't take in a single word of the opening formalities but eventually my solicitor told me it was my turn to speak. She pointed to where I should stand, facing the judge. My dad was behind me and I couldn't see him which was probably better and I started to read from the sheet of paper I had written out.

I took a deep breath. I was shaking like a leaf. I looked at my solicitor and she gave me an encouraging smile.

I started reading from the first sheet:

'In this statement, I simply intend to express and explain the horror I had to endure by a repulsive person I once knew as a loving father. My father should have protected me, but in reality, he was the one I needed protecting from.'

After those first few lines I felt the tears welling up in my eyes. This was tough but I was determined to get through it.

'He was supposed to be my father, someone who loves me unconditionally and protects me from the world and all the bad things out there. He was supposed to keep me safe.
We all need our parents in our lives. A mom and dad, to direct us the right way, show us right from wrong, to help us and guide us through life and protect us from what the world will throw our way.
I begged him many times just to be the father I always wanted. I begged for a family. I begged for him to let my mom into my life.'

I could feel the sweat running down my back and my father's eyes must have been burning into me, cursing every word I spoke. But I continued.

'When I was young I watched my friends and I was jealous of them, because to me they had perfect families. They had family days out, ate as a family at the dinner table while they discussed their days with one another. They had nice family pictures to show to everyone, went on shopping trips and family holidays together. They had everything I could have only ever dream of.
My father was a good father in many respects, I have a lot to thank him for. He kept me healthy, worked

hard to pay for my sporting activities and things I enjoyed. He kept a roof over my head and food on the table. He made sure I had a good education, even when I wasn't in school. He provided home-schooling and made sure I had a good knowledge of life.

My father was there for my first steps and my first words. He took me to my first day at nursery, preschool, primary school, and even secondary school. He made sure I had a clean school uniform every morning, all my equipment and a healthy packed lunch for the day. He even learned how to do girls' hairstyles and plaits so he could do my hair for school. My father watched me grow from a baby to a young girl. But that wasn't enough for him.

As much as my father seemed to do so well for a single father, that wasn't the case, because behind closed doors, things were very different. A lot of parents give their children a tap on the hand or on their bottom if they'd been naughty, but my father took it to another level and he tortured me. My father hurt me. Hurt me is an understatement.

I was his little girl, his princess, how could he have treated me the way he did? What did I do so wrong to him?

From the first moment he laid his hands on me the way he shouldn't have; he changed my life. Everything changed. Sometimes I lie awake at night just staring at the ceiling thinking about how my innocence is no longer mine to keep. The words he used to say to me were bitter, heartless, brutal and cruel. Words no person deserves to be called, let alone a child. He abused me physically and sexually, but above all he abused me mentally.

He would sometimes sit there all smug, while I sat in terrified silence wondering what his next move would be. He would turn around and call me a stupid bitch, he'd tell me that I deserved to die, that I was a worthless whore. I'd lower my head silently, trying to hold back the tears and suddenly he'd hit me in the face. That would often be the start of a whole night's torture. He made me feel so weak and small using those vile words and by hitting me, but he always wanted more. The words and the hitting were never enough.

Never did I realise that it was all part of an elaborate plan to break me.

You made me play games with you. You called it roleplay. Roleplay between a father and his little daughter should be like the games I played with my friends where we pretended to be actors in a soap opera. The roleplay games I played with you were torturous nightmares. You made me drink alcohol and wear short slutty dresses and you made me dance over you while you tore my clothes off . I should have known really, too good to be true! You didn't want to be a 'father' you wanted me to be your 'doll'.

You pounded out my soul while I cried and stared at the ceiling, wondering when it was going to stop. Or the games in the woods? Hide and seek you say? Let's go down to the woods and play on the rope swing you say? Just another one of your fantasies. You weren't even afraid of dog walkers passing by on the other side of the bushes. I was hoping they would hear me crying or begging or trying to scream, but nothing! Nobody came to save me. You didn't care at all. Tearing my clothes off me, in the cold

dirty woods, your hand tightly covering my mouth, the dirty sludgy mud getting under my nails. The excruciating pain you caused me.
Is this really all I was worth to you? Just a young girl you could use and abuse? Did you forget I was your daughter? Or even that I was human? Did you not think about my feelings? Did this not matter to you?
All the times you recorded yourself raping and abusing me. The pictures you took of me in tears while you made me pose as if I was some sort of sex model.
You watched me scream, cry and beg for you to stop while you got off on it? Did you enjoy watching the videos over and over again? Did it satisfy you and your sick and twisted mind? All the times you made me watch them over again, putting me through the torment.
You didn't just do it once or twice, you put me through the pain day in, day out for three-quarters of my life.'

I heard someone gasp in the public gallery and someone else was sobbing. Let that sink in, I thought to myself. Yes, three quarters of my life I have been abused. Not for a week or two, or months or even just a couple of years. Three quarters of my life.
The tears were rolling down my cheeks now. I wanted to sit down; I wanted to collapse onto the floor; I wanted someone to walk over to me and say that's enough. No one came.

'Sometimes it wasn't once a day or even twice, try three, four or five. There have been occasions where it would be all day... Why? Why me? What did I ever do so wrong?

You took it all away from me, my innocence, my childhood, my life. You made me feel so small. Unwanted, unloved, worthless and pathetic. For so long I have walked around with my head hung low, feeling ashamed. Constant feeling of everyone looking at me like I am the weird girl with a baby by her father. You made me feel like I was trapped in a cage I would never be able to get out of. The constant feeling as though death would be the answer. Not wanting to live this horrid life. I never asked for it so why should I have to live with it? I don't even know what love is or how to love. This is all because of you. You ruined me and who I should be. You took my childhood away and that I will never be able to get back. I missed out on being a kid and doing what kids do. I mean all the games children play, you turned some of them into something that should never have even crossed your mind. I couldn't even play with my dolls like I could when I was really little, why? Because I would play with them after you've 'done your act'.'

That was it. I couldn't take any more and the floodgates opened and I couldn't see the words and I couldn't speak. Someone came and led me away towards where my solicitor sat and she put an arm around me to comfort me. She said I had done really well. My auntie came from the public gallery to read the rest of my statement. A week before the sentencing hearing we arranged that if I was unable to speak, my auntie would help me out. I watched as she lifted the last sheet of paper up in front of her face and started to read. I knew it was just a few more lines and that it would soon all be over.

'I would play with my dolls to try and block out what you had just done, with tears falling down my face. This is not love, you don't hurt the ones you love. I couldn't be me. You didn't really care about me. When did you ever really tell me you were proud of me? You never killed me physically, but you made me feel as though I had died many years ago.
The abuse has set my life on the wrong course and destroyed the normal childhood and teenage years that everyone deserves. I feared the consequences of disclosure because I love my dad. I know what he did was wrong, but I grew up with my dad by my side. I just wanted him to get help to make him better but unfortunately that never happened and it has come to this. It's come to me having a baby and to the father being my dad and to him being sentenced and my life falling apart.'

My auntie lowered the paper, sort of nodded at the judge and walked away back over to where she had been sitting. My solicitor leaned over and said it was time for sentencing. Judge Stuart Rafferty didn't smile. I remember looking him and thinking he was so very old and I remember one of the first things he said.
'You took your daughter's life.'
He said my dad would be jailed for life, with a minimum term of 15 years.
Judge Rafferty said, 'It is difficult to find words that could properly describe the extent of your deprivation and the damage that that deprivation has caused, not to a stranger but to your own

daughter. Children do not ask to be born, children are entitled to expect the best from their parents, in terms of care and parental love, that they can possibly receive. You gave your daughter a warped variation of that, a variation that suited you, not her and, although I know you have to serve a prison sentence for that, the sentence you imposed upon her is a far greater one.'

Judge Rafferty said that my father had consigned me to a life of darkness.

'She loved you, as any child loves its parents, and although people may think it strange, she loves you still - that's what children do.'

And then Judge Rafferty was finished.

I remember thinking fifteen years, is that all?

It was over. There were people moving about behind the glass. Dad stood and it dawned on me that they were taking him to prison and in that moment it was not what I wanted. I stood up and ran towards him. Someone grabbed me, people were stopping me from getting to him.

'I love you Dad!' I shouted, 'and I miss you!'

There were more hands on me. I wanted to fight them, I wanted to break free and get to Dad. I looked straight at him. He looked straight at me, and there was no reaction. Nothing.

He looked over to the public gallery to where Mom and my aunties sat. He smirked at them and then he was gone.

My father is incapable of feeling guilt. Even in Derby Crown Court while he pleaded guilty to raping his daughter, there was no remorse and no emotion in his eyes.

But looking back on that day, I have analysed everything my father did in court. Or rather I have analysed what he didn't do. While he pleaded guilty there was no explanation of why he had done what he had, he didn't put his hands up and take responsibly for his actions nor did he address me at any time and tell me he was sorry. He kept his mouth shut and that made me angry. I know he only pleaded guilty so that he could get a sentence reduction.

Just days before my father kidnapped me, he knew it was just a matter of time before he was arrested and he knew it would soon be over. I remember the day so clearly, almost like it was yesterday. Late at night, he sat at the edge of his bed, hung his head down low and told me how sorry he was. He told me then he would be going away for a long time.
He said, 'but I will be out by the time I am fifty and I promise you everything will be okay.'

I wanted my father to stand up in court and apologise to me in public, just like he had apologised in private that night. I wanted him to admit his guilt in front of the world, not sit there with his mouth shut while his solicitor read out a statement.

23

They Tried to Silence Me

I can't begin to describe how difficult this has been for me to write a book. It has been one of the hardest things I have ever had to face up to because at times I had to relive events all over again. I know that Ken Scott, my writing coach, was sometimes tearing his hair out over me, as was my publisher. I'd switch off my phone when I didn't want to talk about things or even worse, when I could see it was Scotty or the publisher trying to reach me, I'd know they wanted more words from me and I'd cut them off as I just couldn't face up to them. Thankfully, they were very patient with me. There were times I simply disappeared for many weeks and buried my head in the sand, taking the line of least resistance, knowing that if they couldn't speak to me then I didn't have to talk about it. I ignored the WhatsApp messages and the emails. I texted an odd message saying I was in a poor reception area or that my phone was playing up. The process itself wasn't difficult, because it was fairly straight forward and I was learning a new skill - writing - that I mostly enjoyed. I'd write up my notes chapter by chapter and Scotty would call me on WhatsApp or message me. We'd go over the notes, he'd ask me to do a rewrite and then he would look at the entire chapter. I would study the chapter notes and comments and he'd point out the good writing and the bad writing and the idea was that my next chapter would be better than the previous one. And it worked. By the time we had completed about seven chapters I read the twenty thousand words again. My God! I thought, have I really written all that? If I say so myself, I was very pleased with my achievement. Scotty told me not to get too cocky, because we'd still need to do a complete rewrite on the book and I realised there was more writing a book than I thought.

It was the content that eventually got to me, particularly as I progressed beyond those first twenty thousand words - chapter 8 onwards. We were now getting on to the violence and the abuse and the more I wrote about it, the more it all came back to me and I was living it all over again. I had locked it all up in a secure place and someone had unlocked it and let it all out. I sank into a severe depression at one stage, wondering if writing a book was such a good idea after all. I knew it had to come out but suddenly I wanted to leave it be. I was back in the police interview suites again and they were asking me some awful questions and wanting me to go into the most graphic details that I wanted to keep to myself. And yet it wasn't like that writing this book because Scotty wasn't looking for intimate details, he was more interested in the episodes of abuse that he kind of sensed I was keeping to myself, things I hadn't disclosed to anyone, especially not to the police. There's a lesson for the police to learn here because their interviews were horrendous, indescribable ordeals and even though the policewomen were softly spoken and kind and brought me anything I wanted and cups of tea by the bucket full they handled me wrong. Scotty was covering the same sort of questions but they were different in the way they were asked and not once did he push me to repeat myself over and over again. Once I had supplied the notes, or messaged a paragraph on WhatsApp, or spoke to him over the phone, that was it. The worst bit with the police was repeat, repeat, repeat. I can't think for the life of me why they made me go through it all so many times, all the while filming it and recording it and taking notes. Perhaps if they had kept to only asking questions once, then I may have felt like opening up a bit and bringing the other things into the light. I know I'm probably being unfair to the police, but in reality I blame them for much of this because they were in a position of authority, part of the overall big network of institutions that had let me down. In many respects they had failed me too.

It was suggested that I should fly over to Spain where Scotty lives. So that's what I did. The publisher was there too, a nice South African lady whose idea it was to bring me to Spain. She thought it would be more productive to meet face to face and they booked me into a hotel for two weeks. I settled into a pleasant routine of work and surprised myself with just how much I enjoyed it. It was hard, difficult work and long hours and at times it was too much for me. Some afternoons I crept away to my room and told Scotty that I wasn't feeling very well. From a health point of view I was fine but my head was in a bad place. He said it didn't matter and told me to take a notepad and a pen with me and to 'do what I can.' That happened a few times. I stayed in my room and tried to see the notes through the tears. I got through it and was determined not to let anyone down. I rallied and made it down to the breakfast meetings with the publisher and Scotty every morning. Some days we worked right through from breakfast to early evening and one day we clocked up 14 hours. I loved Spain, I loved the way people treated me normally and it was nice to walk the streets among strangers, knowing that they knew nothing about me, about who I was, or what I had been through. As we neared the end of the second week they told me I had written over fifty thousand words in total. My God! I battled through it and although the book wasn't complete Scotty told the publisher he had enough of the story in note format, it was just a case of 'bringing it all together.' I was sad when the publisher took me to the airport and yet optimistic that there could be a bright future ahead of me as a writer and motivational speaker. I was formulating plans in my head; I wanted to move to Spain where nobody knew me, where I felt I could make a clean start, somewhere where my father couldn't find me when he eventually got released. The book was almost there and if it sold well who knows what might happen? Fortis Publishing had placed me on their highest royalty rate and promised that they would entertain the possibility of a second book. I was buzzing and during the flight over to the UK I made copious notes on what was to be my final chapter.

When the plane touched down I checked my work and found that I had written almost two thousand words. As I walked through the terminal building, I telephoned Scotty and told him that we were nearly there.

'Brilliant,' he said, 'I just need to speak to Derby Crown Court and get the full list of your father's convictions and his sentences then we are good to go.'

I couldn't quite believe it, I had pulled off the impossible and written a book (with a little help, I hasten to add,) and it was going to be published!

Little did I know what a certain judge was about to do to me.

Scotty called Derby Crown Court and was told to put his request in writing. He did so the same day, stating in the email that he requested the exact charges Shane Clifton had been charged with and his convictions. The purpose he explained, was for a book that he was writing with Clifton's daughter Shannon.

For two weeks he heard nothing and wrote again.

The following emails have been copied verbatim.

Good Evening,

I telephoned Derby Crown Court two weeks ago relating to information about Shane Clifton to be told you didn't give information out over the phone. You said I needed to

put my request in writing, which I did.
I had an automatic reply but to date no information has been forthcoming. Can you please advise how long these enquiries normally take?
To remind you, I require the exact charges Shane Clifton was charged with (2015) and what he was convicted of.

The reply came few days later.

Good Afternoon,

This request has been referred to HHJ Rafferty QC, who heard the case at Derby Crown Court. His Honour does not regularly sit at this court and so the matter had to be forwarded on to him.

Scotty phoned me and read the contents of the reply. My heart skipped a beat when he mentioned Judge Rafferty.
Why was he involved? I thought to myself. This was the judge who had served my father with a life sentence with a minimum term of fifteen years. However, it appears that the Judge, when sentencing my father to a minimum of 15 years, may have made a mistake. When defendants plead guilty to offences they are usually given 'credit' for those guilty pleas, which means their sentence is reduced from what it would have been if they had been found guilty following a trial. I believe they call it plea bargaining. In principle it works most of the time because giving evidence in a trial can be distressing for the victims. In my case especially so, because I was just a child. So, my father pleaded guilty and the theory was that he should get 'credit,' because he had done such an

honourable thing and saved me the trauma of testifying at trial. When I was initially notified of this 'credit' that my father had received, I was livid. He couldn't possibly have gone to trial and expected a not guilty verdict, because the DNA from my son proved beyond doubt that he was the father. I can imagine the discussion that would have taken place between my father and his lawyer.

Dad would have said, 'I'm pleading not guilty.'

His Lawyer would have said, 'you're having a laugh mate, have you forgotten about the DNA results?'

'Oh shit! Yea, I had.'

'Exactly,' his lawyer would have said, 'now, we are going to plead guilty and I'll get a few years knocked off your sentence for it.'

'Sounds like a good plan,' Dad would have said.

And that is exactly what happened.

On 23 April 2015, Dad was sentenced to life imprisonment with a minimum of 15 years. The sentence was amended the day after to a minimum of 10 years.

Five years reduction. It defies logic that Judge Rafferty decided that to plead guilty to an offence that was just about as black and white as it can possibly be, warrants a reduction of five years from a sentence. Maybe he didn't have a choice, because maybe that's what the law says, but either way, it stinks. Even now when I read this again it seems like something from a fiction novel. It gets worse. My Dad then tried to appeal the minimum ten-year term and his legal team argued the ten-year minimum sentence was harsh. Thankfully, the Court of Appeal did not accept what my father's legal team were saying and kept the sentence as it was, ten years minimum. To this day I still lie awake at night and relive the judge's 'Minimum Sentence.' Is it any wonder that when Ken Scott mentioned his name I started shaking like a leaf? I understand that his hands were tied by the UK legal system and that it was the maximum sentence he could have given my dad, but it still disgusts me that this is the best that could be done.

A week later another reply from Derby Crown Court:

His Honour has directed:

'No explanation has been provided for the making of the enquiry or the purpose for which the information is required. Accordingly the application is refused.'

Scotty received this reply nearly a month after our initial enquiry. I had been wondering what the hold-up was, because I was back on track after my long emotional absence from the book and now it suddenly looked as if things had ground to a halt again and this time it wasn't my fault. During a conversation with the publisher she explained that the information from Derby Crown Court was the only item holding things up.

Scotty wrote again.

My original email clearly stated that I simply required the original charges Shane Clifton faced, and of what he was eventually convicted. I stated also that I needed this information for a book I am working on with Shannon

Clifton, his daughter whom he abused. I simply need to know the EXACT charges and convictions, I believe this information is in the public domain anyway but cannot find specifics.
Is it easier if I ask Shannon Clifton to contact you?

And finally, a week later, the email arrived.

The information can be released to you is as follows –

Count 1 *Rape a girl under 13 – pleaded not guilty – count to lie on file*
Count 2 *Rape a girl under 13 – pleaded not guilty – count to lie on file*
Count 3 *Rape a girl under 13 – pleaded not guilty – count to lie on file*
Count 4 *Rape a girl under 13 – pleaded guilty*
Count 5 *Rape a girl under 13 – pleaded guilty*
Count 6 *Rape a girl under 13 – pleaded guilty*
Count 7 *Sexually assault a girl under 13 – penetration – pleaded not guilty – count to lie on file*
Count 8 *Rape a girl 13/14/15 years of age – pleaded guilty*
Count 9 *Rape a girl 13/14/15 years of age – pleaded guilty*

Sentence
Count 4 *– Life imprisonment with a specified minimum term of 10 years - Discretionary Life Sentence – Sex offenders register indefinitely – Sexual Harm Prevention Order until further order – Barring list*
Count 5 *- Life imprisonment with a specified minimum term of 10 years concurrent*
Count 6 *- Life imprisonment with a specified minimum term of 10 years concurrent*
Count 8 *- Life imprisonment with a specified minimum term of 10 years concurrent*

Count 9 *- Life imprisonment with a specified minimum term of 10 years concurrent*

The defendant lodged an appeal against sentence in 2015. The appeal was refused however the minimum term in the case should have been expressed as a minimum term of 10 years less 181 days spent in custody on remand.

Great, Scotty thought, now we can get this book finished, tidied up and published. But no, at the bottom of the email there was this footnote:

HHJ Rafferty QC also made the following comment.

'The fact that the victim is collaborating with him in the preparation of a book concerning what befell her has the inevitable effect of driving a coach and horses through the original restraining order, which nonetheless remains in force in respect of both her child and herself.'
Can I also remind you that reporting restrictions are in force until further order and restrict publicity in respect of the youth victim. This includes publication of the youths name, address, school or anything else that may identify them, including a picture.

Unknown to me, Scotty immediately had a meeting with the publisher. This was serious, it appeared that the judge was blocking publication of the book by way of a reporting restriction which was still in force from when I was still a minor in 2015. This would prevent any publication of anything relating to my story. He phoned me immediately after the meeting.

'It's bad news Shannon, the publishers have spoken

to their lawyers and we can't proceed with the book until the judge lifts the order.'

I was in tears; absolutely devasted. I had put my life and soul into this book, thinking and believing it was my one and only opportunity to make a fresh start and do something important with my life. After my return from Spain, I had been active on social media, I had a new purpose in life and I had been talking to other victims of sexual and physical abuse, writing articles and blogging that whatever has happened to you it's not the end of the world, you can still survive.

I didn't agree with the judge and I was adamant that he was not going to silence me. I wasn't a child anymore and besides; I had waived my right to anonymity nearly a year ago and several magazine and newspapers had already interviewed me and published articles about me. My story had been published several times and other media outlets had picked up on the news and reprinted it.

Scotty agreed to try again.

He wrote to the court, wondered if the judge was aware of all of the facts.

Can I respectfully ask once again, is the QC aware that 1. Shannon is now 19 years of age and not a child 2. That she waived her right to anonymity a year ago? 3. It is Shannon who is writing her own book?

The correspondence was now coming thick and fast. Scotty copied me in on the latest email from Derby Crown Court.

In response to your email, HHJ Rafferty QC made the

following comment regarding the press restriction on a previous occasion when a press request was submitted to the Court –

'The order was made with good reason, namely, the protection of the child victim and the child she gave birth to as a result of the offences committed against her.'

The press restrictions for the victim and her child remain in force until further order. (Indefinitely.)

I was furious, the judge was referring to me as a child; clearly he had not done his calculations. My father was convicted in 2015 and I was fifteen at the time, but this is 2019 and I'm not a minor anymore. Couldn't the man count? I was furious and determined and I was ready to jump on the bus and go to Derby Crown Court myself. After everything I had been through, how dare he try to gag me! Scotty emailed again in a desperate last attempt to beg the judge to reconsider the order.

Judge Rafferty replied again and this time I detected that he was well pissed off with my writing coach.

As I have made plain on a number of occasions now, and do not expect to have to reiterate, the restriction order that I made was intended to provide lifetime protection not merely to the child complainant of familial sexual abuse but further, and of even greater importance, the child of that unlawful relationship. It is not open to the mother to waive her entitlement to that protection, whatever the reason for that might be, particularly when to do so patently would jeopardise the protection by it afforded to her child. To do otherwise would place her in contempt of the court's order, as it would anyone who aid, abetted, counselled or procured her to take such a course. To embark upon the production of a book without having ascertained the legal position first was a wholly inappropriate course to have taken in my judgement. There is no valid basis for a review of the order and accordingly it stands.

I decided to go to Derby Crown Court. We all still felt that the court and the judge were unaware of the exact nature of the case and why I wanted to write this book. I felt that if I had a chance to sit with someone in an official capacity and explain myself that they might lift the restriction and I would be able to tell my story.

I made an appointment at the court and showed up for it, but when it was my time to be seen they said that I would need to send an email. I asked if it was possible to speak with the judge.

It was not.

And so, I sent an email laying out my reasons for writing the book and asked Judge HHJ Rafferty QC to please reconsider.

I received a reply almost identical to the one Scotty had, with a few bolt-ons and a bit of advice at the end.

As I have made plain on a number of occasions now, and do not expect to have to reiterate, the restriction order that I made was intended to provide lifetime protection not merely to the child complainant of familial sexual abuse but further, and of even greater importance, the child of that unlawful relationship. It is not open to the mother to waive her entitlement to that protection, whatever the reason for that might be, particularly when to do so patently would jeopardise the protection by it afforded to her child. To do otherwise would place her in contempt of the court's order, as it would anyone who aid, abetted, counselled or procured her to take such a course. To embark upon the production of a book without having ascertained the legal position first was a wholly inappropriate course to have taken in my judgement. There is no valid basis for a review of the order and accordingly it stands.

It is not open to you to waive your entitlement to protection and you will be in contempt of court as the order remains in place. You would be advised to seek legal advice.

He wasn't changing his mind; it was as clear as bottled water. Coincidently, that evening Scotty sent over the first completed draft of the book. The next morning I went to a shop and printed the 120 pages and took it to bed with me that night. Once again, I relived the horrors I had gone through. I finished it at six in the morning and then slept until about ten. I drank a few coffees and tried to eat something but I couldn't keep anything down.

I picked up the book again and randomly read one of the chapters again. Had I really written that, I thought to myself.

Apart from my son, it was my greatest achievement in life. I had written a damned good book that people had to read because if I could survive the nightmare I had gone through then others could too. How many young girls had been raped and abused and put through similar abuse?

This isn't a handbook or a 'how to survive,' manual,

but it it's a book that details my abuse, my torture, my cries for help that fell on deaf ears. It's testament to the fact I had lived through it, then had the courage to put it down on paper.

And now they wanted to stop me.

I talked to my friends and I spoke to Scotty and my publisher. The consensus was that the best person to get this restriction lifted was me and so, that same day I sat down and planned what I was going to do. There was no way HHJ Rafferty QC was going to silence me.

I sent him an email via Derby Crown Court.

I appreciate that you 'intended to provide lifetime protection', but I disagree that I don't have the right to waive it now that I'm an adult. I don't need you to speak for me anymore.

You may not want to 'reiterate' and this may be a hassle for you, but this matter is not going away and you need to address it.

After I was taken into care at 13, I spent the next 5 years of my life being sent from pillar to post and the list of institutions that let me down during that time is long and depressing. I was severely traumatised and during all this time I never received any psychological counselling worth mentioning. I still don't get any mental health care from the state and I can't afford private help. The only thing I can do now is to face my demons and to tell my story.

About being held in contempt of court as you threaten in your email. Here are links to some of the online newspaper articles about me:

(Here I supplied links to online articles that appeared in Metro, The Mirror, The Daily Mail, The Sun, The Express).

The Metro article alone has been shared on Facebook 10,500 times.

There are many more articles and as you can see, the cat is out the bag. I have also appeared in magazine articles and one of the big TV stations have asked to do a documentary about my story.

You say I should have asked about the legal position before I started to write the book. How was I to know you had decided I wasn't allowed to tell the story about my own life? Why would it ever have occurred to me? The first I heard of it was when the writer I asked to help me with the book contacted the court about my father's convictions.

'It is not open to you to waive your entitlement to protection and you will be in contempt of court as the order remains in place. You would be advised to seek legal advice.'

I'm a 19-year old unemployed student, how do you propose I afford legal advice? I disagree that I don't have the right to waive my entitlement to protection.

I may not have any money for legal advice, but I do have 5000 friends and followers on Facebook and I know how to use social media. Judge, if you refuse to waive this order and you hold me in contempt of court, you can't fine me because I don't have money so you will have to send me to prison. Do you want to be the judge who sends a 19-year old rape victim to prison, especially after reducing her serial rapist father's life sentence to 10 years? Speaking of my father – I'm also writing this book so I can get money together to leave the UK before he gets out of prison because I'm terrified of him. By the way, did you consider my 'lifetime protection' when you reduced his life sentence to only 10 years? You may have the Derby Crown Court on your side, but on whose side do you think the court of public opinion will be?

I am writing my book and I will publish it, even if I have to put it page by page on Facebook. Will you hold Facebook in contempt of court? More than half of my supporters are outside the UK so I can simply publish the book in America and tell the UK buyers to order the Kindle version on Amazon.com. What do you think it will do to my book sales if people know it's banned in the UK? Will you hold Amazon in contempt as well?

My friends are telling me to get a Facebook petition going to collect signatures demanding that you leave me alone. The petition will be addressed to you personally. Women all over the world are coming forward to shine the light on their sexual abuse and if you try to stop me from telling my own story, I will cause a public outcry over it.

About my little boy. I'm not a psychopath so of course I'm not going to name him in the book or give any information that will lead back to him. Anyway, it's been all over the newspapers that I gave birth to a son so it's hardly news anymore.

I therefore ask that you rescind the protection order asap so that I may get on with my life. Please let me know when it's done.

Regards,
Shannon Clifton

I confess when I pressed 'send' I was a bundle of nerves and quite scared at what I had written to a man of his stature. And yet I was determined and ready for anything. I felt empowered by what I had written and stronger than I had felt for some time. I was ready for the fight of my life and I was convinced the judge would let the wrath of God reign down upon me.

A few days later we received this reply from Judge Rafferty.

In light of the full history now disclosed by Miss Clifton, it is clear that the order I made can no longer serve any useful purpose. Accordingly, it is rescinded with immediate effect and I shall take no action on the serial breaches of it. Therefore there are no longer any press restrictions.

Halleluiah!
I had won! My determination and sheer will to publish my book had paid off! It once again confirmed to me that it is never too late to start again. I was about to publish a book, to become an author. It was for real! I picked up my phone and called Scotty.

24

They All Failed Me

Around the time I started my book, one of my friends phoned me and told me about an article by Russell Pollard, an independent news journalist at a website called Derby News (derbynews.org.co.uk). Although I had never met Mr Pollard, I did remember that he had contacted me for an interview some time back but I had politely declined because I didn't know him.

Mr Pollard had written about and he had clearly done his research and as I read the article, I couldn't help but be impressed with his knowledge of my case and the forthright, passionate manner in which he was writing. Almost immediately, he mentions my nemesis, Judge Rafferty:

April 2015, during the sentencing of Shane Clifton, a Derby man who had repeatedly raped his daughter from

the age of 6 through to 13, Judge Stuart Rafferty stated 'You took your daughter's life.'
His daughter, Shannon, first became pregnant by him at the age of 11; Clifton was so angry when he found out that he beat her so badly that Shannon miscarried. He had a history of family violence; he was sent to prison when Shannon was five for harming her mother.
In the Derby Telegraph article on the case, it reported that; 'The abuse only stopped once her school alerted the authorities that the teenager was pregnant.'
This was October 2014. The baby was born a few weeks later. The article continues:
'The judge said the man consigned his daughter to 'a life of darkness,' making her lead an isolated life so that she had no-one to turn to.'
How could a teenager, living in the heart of Chaddesden, who was regularly absent from different schools, isolated from the community, and then 9 months pregnant, be overlooked by the very authorities who should be there to protect her. Was it really the case that the first time that the Council had been notified of any concerns regarding Shannon's safety was when the school noticed that she was pregnant?

Mr Pollard had asked the million-dollar question: was it the first time the council had known about any concerns relating to my abuse?
He answered the question himself and continued:

No!
Neighbours had been trying to raise the alarm for years beforehand, but it seems that they were ignored by Councillors, Council Officers, the Police, and the local MP.

And then the article took on a new twist and I sat back in utter astonishment as the journalist revealed and copied out a series of emails that I knew nothing about. It was the first time I had heard of some of the people he was referring to. It was also fairly obvious that certain neighbours were aware that something serious had been going on for a number of years. I felt sick in the stomach as I reread the line - 'Neighbours had been trying to raise the alarm for years.'

I read on:

In an email exchange between a Neighbour and a Derby Homes Housing and Neighbourhood Manager on ***25 July 2013*** *(15 months before the school alerted the authorities) the Neighbour writes:*
'Hi xxxx, I think you are a very brave man (remember baby P). I would like this all put on record that we have warned you about all that has happened next door (for 18 months) this is a disaster waiting to happen. If anything happens to me or my family or the 13-year-old girl next door I will hold you personally responsible for what happens, as you seem to be in charge of a bunch of morons'

The response from the Derby Homes manager on the **26 July 2013**:

'xxxx I have, as I stated in my last email to you, I reported your concerns regarding the daughter of your neighbour to the social services department......As I am sure you will agree we all have a responsibility where children may be at risk.'

On the **9th September 2013** the neighbour emailed Chris Williamson MP, ex-Cllr Sara Bolton, and Maria Murphy, MD of Derby Homes. His email started by saying:

'You three are our last port of call.'

He proceeded to explain how Shane Clifton had removed support walls from the house (A Derby Homes property), removed gas fires, allegations about drug dealing and other damage to the property. He then continues:

'The second thing is that his 13-year-old daughter Shannon has not been to school for over a year. We have been in touch with the Council on a number of occasions....We have also been in contact with social services about Shannon going back to school. We spoke to CB, she stated that this was on-going....'

The email finished with a plea:

'Remember baby P. We are not the sort of people to send emails like this. It has took (sic) a lot of soul searching to send this.'

Ex-Cllr Sara Bolton followed up by responding on **9 September 2013:**

'Thank you for your email below and I am alarmed by the contents.
I have to say that this is the first contact I have had about the property involved so will act quickly.
Please rest assured I will do what I can and I apologise for

the lack of response to date.'

Oh great, Ex-Cllr Sara Bolton, you seem to be concerned about the property, that really reassures me. Sara Bolton said, and I quote, 'I will do what I can.'

That was on 9 September. I have never heard the name Sara Bolton since.

Chris Williamson responded on the **10 September 2013**, by email:

'I know Cllr Sara Bolton has been in touch with you and is going to raise the matters you brought to our attention with the Council's Neighbourhood team. I will follow up Sara's intervention to reinforce the points she is making. Hopefully our joint intervention will bring some improvement in the situation you have been forced to endure.'

This was followed up by a letter from Williamson on the **13th September 2013** on House of Commons letter headed paper.

'I have written to Derby Homes and the Director for Children's Services at Derby City Council regarding the issues you raised. The Police have informed me that they are already investigating this individual and will update me further at a later stage'.

The neighbours received a response from ex-Cllr Sara Bolton on **12 October 2013:**
'Yes I am aware as (you) email me on a regular basis.

Derby Homes and the Children and Young People team in Derby City Council are dealing with matters'

I detect a definite irritation from ex-Cllr Sara Bolton in this response. She seems a little put out that this individual emails her on a regular basis.

In an email from Clare Mehrbani (Head of Housing Management - Derby Homes) on **14th October 2013**, to the Neighbour following up on previous concerns:

'Your concerns about the schooling of the tenants daughter have been forwarded to the relevant MAT (Multi-Agency Team) within Derby City Council. Derby Homes are unable to comment further on this due to issues of privacy but can assure you that your concerns have reached the appropriate authority'
This email was copied to ex-Cllr Sara Bolton, the MD of Derby Homes, and Sgt Woods of Derbyshire Constabulary.

All this correspondence took place before I was pregnant in 2019. I could feel the bile rising up in my throat and I started to feel sick. The people and the departments who knew or at least suspected, what had been going on with me were all listed in the article. Derby Homes, the school authorities, Neighbourhood Management, Chris Williamson MP, Sara Bolton, Maria Murphy, Social Services, the Director for Children's Services, the police, Sgt Woods and Andrew Bunyon, the Children & Young People's team as well as the Multi Agency Team and Clare Mehrbani.
There were dozens of people or departments who

were warned, who should have acted.
Mr Pollard's article continued.

On **10 December 2013**, Chief Inspector Dick Hargreaves wrote to the Neighbour on a number of points of complaint about Mr Clifton. He stated:

'The allegations about the welfare of Mr Clifton's daughter have previously been reported to us through Sgt Woods and she has made the appropriate referrals to the education / social services for action as they deem appropriate.'

Despite many assurances, the neighbours did not feel that any progress was being made and that Shannon's safety was still a major concern. They wrote a letter, dated ***31 August 2014****, to Andrew Bunyan the Director of Children's Services titled* ***'Child in Danger.'***

'We are very, very concerned about the girl who lives next door, her name is Shannon Clifton....We have been down to the Social Services office on Osmaston Road, Derby, they told us she has a social worker and lots of problems with the family.

Really? Social Services disclosed this confidential information to one of my neighbours?

They live in a two bedroomed house managed by Derby Homes only one of the bedrooms is being used. As we have discussed many times, she has hardly been to school for 7-8 years, we know she has been expelled from at least 3 schools....'

This was replied to by Maureen Darbon (Acting Service Director - Early Intervention and Integrated safeguarding) on **1 September 2014**.

'In relation to the concerns you have expressed regarding the child's wellbeing I assure you these have been taken seriously and will be followed up….'

I couldn't believe what I was reading: 'Child in Danger', Maureen Darbon's reply. And all that time, while the abuse kept coming, the violence escalated and the rapes became commonplace I thought that nobody knew, nobody cared. I wiped a tear from my eye as I tried to hold back the floodgates. They did know, everybody bloody knew! They did nothing, the pencil pushing jobsworths!

Russell Pollard wrote:

Despite all of these promises of action - the abuse didn't stop.
In **January 2014** they met with Kevin Murphy at Leesbrook School in Chaddesden. He was the Strategic Director, Safeguarding, Child Protection and Attendance. Previously he had been the Head of Service, Early Intervention and Integrated Safeguarding with Derby City Council. They raised with Mr Murphy their concerns over safeguarding and the relationship between Clifton and his daughter. He committed to inform the Council through his contacts as, 'I am concerned about her well-being.'

A few months after Clifton's case came to court in **2015,** the Neighbours contacted Kevin Murphy to highlight the outcome of the case. He responded:

'...I was warned off talking to you again...I did see the case come to court and I was aware that this was the gentleman in question which did vindicate all that you both said. I did wonder why you were not believed and ***why the cover up****. I have worked very closely with the Police over the years, especially with regard to children and still cannot believe this was allowed to happen. I hope you are both now ok following this. I was told not to interfere as this was a very dangerous man and that they did not want the school bringing into the matter.'*

Reading the last paragraph finished me and I collapsed in a flood of tears. What the hell did he mean 'he was warned off talking to the neighbours', what did he mean by a 'cover up?' And worst of all 'I was told not to interfere as this was a very dangerous man and that they did not want the school bringing into the matter?'

25

Final Thoughts and Moving On

Towards the end of this book, Scotty said that I needed to finish the last few chapters on a high. He said I had to be inspirational and talk about the future and try and put the past behind me. It's easy for you to say that, I joked.

Sometimes life shows us things we never thought it would. The years have passed by in the blink of an eye but it doesn't stop the nightmares of the life I once lived. I often wake up crying in the middle of the night. Not every night, but most of them and when I wake up it doesn't stop the pain. Flashbacks of the torture I lived through come to me in the darkness and in the light of day. I relive the horrors of my past every day.

As kids we often think we have monsters under our bed, but I'm now an adult and I still think I do. I just have to keep telling myself, 'no, it's just in my head'.

For many years I thought it was all my fault and that what happened to me was because I did something wrong. I wondered why I was wasn't loved. What was so bad about me? There must be a reason why my father would be doing this to me and for years I tortured myself over it. I have scars on my body that I put there myself. Causing pain to my body left me in control, and for a while I wouldn't feel the pain in my head. I've lain in hospital beds almost dying because of what I did to myself. I often thought suicide was the only way out. I thought this pain will never stop; how do I possibly carry on?

I still hurt and I still cry and I have days when I don't want to do anything or talk to anyone.

But now I *am* in control and I don't hurt myself so much anymore. I don't put myself through all that pain if I can help it. It's okay to be sad sometimes and it's okay to cry, but what isn't okay is hurting myself and giving in to the demons inside my head. It is not okay to think it's your fault because let me tell you, it's not your fault. I'm still recovering but I'm stronger now and I know that what my father did to me was not my fault.

I'm not a victim anymore; I tell myself every hour of every day: I'm a survivor.

Believe me, there were many times when I nearly didn't finish this project. At times Scotty was tearing his hair out waiting for my next tranche of words while I took writer's block to a new level and sometimes a month would pass before I had the inclination to open my laptop again. I've battled through on this project and at times it was very painful for me even though I knew it had to be done so that I could finish it and move forward. I don't want to keep dwelling on the past.

Earlier this year I started studying towards a degree in forensic psychology at the Open University. I want to see if I can possibly begin to understand what drives people to commit the crimes they do without a shred of empathy for their victims. In my case, my tormentor was a parent, a father I should have trusted, not someone who should have tortured and abused me. My father went against every law in nature where the dominant male should have looked after his brood. I want to know why that happened, it fascinates me and perhaps during the six years I will be enrolled in this course I may get the answers I am looking for.

I may even find a career in this specialised field, who knows. I may be able to help others come to terms with the abuse that they have suffered. I'm well qualified because I have survived and more so, I am willing to write and to talk about my experiences. Growing up in a very dysfunctional family and the things my father has done to me has made me want to know why people do such things and what exactly runs through their mind, before, during and after a particularly vile event.

I really do not know which direction I want to go down professionally, all I do know is that I want to make a success of my life to prove to myself and others that anything is possible. I may write another book, I became a public speaker or I may do something different altogether. For the first time in my life I can look for a future filled with hope and possibility. I look at Elizabeth Smart and Natascha Kampusch who suffered horrific sexual abuse like I have and I can't help but admire them as they stand up in front of large audiences and share their stories.

The more I study life and the more I investigate fathers like Fred West and Josef Fritzl, the more I wonder if perhaps my case isn't just the tip of a huge big iceberg. My own father kept me as a virtual sex slave for nearly ten years and every week we read of another woman who has suffered a similar horror. How many more girls are out there suffering sexual abuse at the hands of their fathers, brothers, uncles or cousins? How many are prisoners in their own homes and have nowhere to turn?
I have a lot of questions to ask my father and I know I will never be able to ask him directly so I've asked Scotty, my writing coach, if he can help in some way. I find it easy to talk to him and during the course of writing this book, I have told him things that I have never told anyone else. He is my therapist and my confidant and I thank him for that. I wonder if the authorities would allow Scotty to go and visit my father in prison. I have so many questions I want to write down for my father and I wonder if he is man enough and compassionate enough to answer them. I want to ask him why he ruined my childhood and hurt me the way he did even though he knew the pain he was putting me through. Perhaps I'm dreaming; why would he give me the answers I'm looking for? He is cunning and deceitful, and I remember that smirk as he was sentenced, when I said I loved and missed him. My mom is convinced that the smirk said, 'look, see how I still control her, look how she still loves me after everything I've done to her.'

I get asked a lot if I am frightened of my father. Of course I am! I fear the day he is released because I know he will blame me and likely come looking for me. Do I think he will kill me? Yes, he has the capability to do that, remember, he killed my unborn child.

A couple of weeks ago, a person in authority, who was involved in my father's case in 2015, gave me some information about him that made my blood run cold. They said my father blamed me for everything. His very words were: 'She just kept getting into my bed. It was a joint process; we knew we had a problem but we didn't know how to stop it.'
How dare he say that! At just six years old I didn't even know what sexual intercourse was, and I because of the excruciating pain it caused, I remember begging him to leave me alone each and every time he forced himself on me. I certainly didn't 'keep getting in his bed,' I wanted to run as far away as I possibly could and I distinctly remember keeping out of his way and hiding from him.
My father also blamed my mother, saying, 'she should never have left her with me.'
When I was younger, I had also blamed my mother. She knew he was abusing me physically, so why did she not take me away from him? Why didn't she come to my rescue? She was my Mom, how hard would it have been? I don't believe she knew the extent of the sexual abuse, after all, it's unimaginable. She had, she said, reported the physical abuse many times, but nothing ever came of it, because Social Care decided to not follow up on the reports or complaints with any actions to remove me from the

care of my dad. In one report, Social Care had replied to my mother that, 'there are no concerns regarding the safety and welfare of the child.' If she ever reads this book, I know it will not make pleasant reading for her. She let me down badly and I think she probably realises that now but then again, we must not forget, she was not the person who abused and hurt me.
It wasn't just a simple matter of going directly to my father. He was a violent psychopath and he had already proved to her how violent he could be towards her. She said that if she had decided to take me away without his knowledge, he would have hunted her down and killed both of us. I accept that she is probably right, but she should have tried. She should have persisted. She's my mother, she should have saved me, it's her duty.

As we approach the end of this book, I can forgive you for thinking that I am a broken girl, and that I could not possibly be fixed. Sometimes, I confess… that is how I feel. I feel as though someone has shattered me into a million pieces, but day by day I try to put the pieces back together, bit by bit. I don't think I will ever be able to piece every bit together, but, as I keep pushing forward, I will eventually get there.

I have had teachers, friends, people in Social Services and the police tell me that they are surprised that I am still here, let alone willing to document my story. Sometimes I wonder too, but then I realize I am stronger than I think. I am not invincible but I am for sure a very strong person. I have been knocked down

so many times but I will always get back up and stand tall and proud. I intend to carry on with my life and make the best out of a bad situation. I always say you should try and take positives out of the negatives and I keep saying to myself, 'I've had a shit start in life… that's all.'
We don't and can't choose how our early life plans out as a child. We can't control our lives as much as you may think you can because things happen that you can't help, or even expect. But you deal with it, you make the most out of your situation whether it is bad or good. I hope to show others out there that no matter what we go through in life there will always be a positive to it all. My positive take on the torture and abuse I endured, is that it made me stronger and more determined and the best revenge is to show my father that he didn't break me and that I went on to have a prosperous and successful life healing myself and helping others.

Many people let me down as a child; dozens who failed me by turning the other cheek and looking the other way. I try not to be bitter and blame them because there was only one person who carried out the abuse against me. But I do want to change things within our society, within our care system. I will never be able to save or help everybody but I intend to try my hardest to help as many people possible all over the world. I will speak out about the horrific things that happened to me in the hope other people will gain the confidence to do the same and I'll tell them that it IS possible to get through it. The memories of what my father did to me will never go away but I will move on. My story isn't a story where the girl lives happily ever after. Nobody who has been raped lives happily ever after. We will never be able to stop people from being raped but at least when it has been proven beyond all reasonable that someone has been damaged in that way, give them the help that they deserve.

Throughout my life, I have been let down miserably by family, the authorities and people close to me but I will survive and I am determined to live each day to my fullest. I am hoping that this book is *stage 2* of my life and if it sells well, I may be able to turn my life around, get off benefits and use the money to help others. So if you're going through a tough time remember you can get through it.

No matter what knocks you down in life, get straight back up and keep getting up until eventually you stay up.

You deserve this life and you deserve to be happy and never ever give up. There's help out there, there are some lovely people around and there are people who care and want to listen. So even in times of loneliness remember there are people you can talk to and lean on, you just need to go find them.

Be heard, be strong and be proud.

Printed in Great Britain
by Amazon

35702743R00137